WALTER LIPPMANN

WALTER LIPPMANN

WALTER LIPPMANN

A Study in Personal Journalism

DAVID ELLIOTT WEINGAST

With an Introduction by
HAROLD L. ICKES

GREENWOOD PRESS, PUBLISHERS
WESTPORT, CONNECTICUT

The quoted material in this book is from:

American Magazine: "Big Business Men of Tomorrow" (April, 1934) and "Security" (May, 1935) by Walter Lippmann. *The American Mercury:* A letter from Herbert Bayard Swope (May, 1945); reprinted by permission of Mr. Swope and *The American Mercury.* *The Atlantic Monthly:* "Scholar In A Troubled World" (August, 1932) by Walter Lippmann; reprinted by permission of Mr. Lippmann. *Christian Century Foundation:* Reprinted from "What Has Happened to Walter Lippmann?" in the issue of September 23, 1936, by permission of the *Christian Century.* *Commonweal:* "Man's Image of Man" (February 13, 1942) by Walter Lippmann; reprinted by permission of *Commonweal. It Seems to Me* by Heywood Broun, copyright, 1935, by Harcourt, Brace & Company, Inc.; used by permission of the publisher. *Drift and Mastery* by Walter Lippmann, copyright, 1914, by Henry Holt & Company, Inc.; used by permission of the publisher. *The New York Herald Tribune:* Permission to quote from Lippmann's column "Today and Tomorrow," and from other articles, granted by The New York Herald Tribune. *The Good Society* by Walter Lippmann, copyright, 1937, by Little, Brown & Company; *U.S. Foreign Policy: Shield of the Republic* by Walter Lippmann, copyright, 1943, by Little, Brown & Company; and *U.S. War Aims* by Walter Lippmann, copyright, 1944, by Little, Brown & Company; used by permission of the publisher. *American Inquisitors* by Walter Lippmann, copyright, 1928, by Walter Lippmann; *A Preface to Morals* by Walter Lippmann, copyright, 1929, by Walter Lippmann; *A Preface to Politics* by Walter Lippmann, copyright, 1933, by Walter Lippmann; *At the Paris Peace Conference* by James T. Shotwell, copyright, 1937, by the Macmillan Company; *John Reed* by Granville Hicks, copyright, 1936, by the Macmillan Company; *Men of Destiny* by Walter Lippmann, copyright, 1927, by Walter Lippmann; *Public Opinion* by Walter Lippmann, copyright, 1922, by Walter Lippmann; *The Method of Freedom* by Walter Lippmann, copyright, 1934, by Walter Lippmann; *The New Imperative* by Walter Lippmann, copyright, 1935, by Walter Lippmann; *The Phantom Public* by Walter Lippmann, copyright, 1925, by Walter Lippmann; and *The Stakes of Diplomacy* by Walter Lippmann, copyright, 1915, by Walter Lippmann; used by permission of the Macmillan Company, publisher. *New Masses:* "Walter Lippmann and Soviet Russia" (August 20, 1935) by Corliss Lamont; and "The Heart of Foreign Policy" (June 29, 1943) by Joseph Starobin. *New Republic:* permission to reprint material from articles appearing over a period of several years granted by the publisher. *Saturday Review of Literature:* "Walter Lippmann" (January 7, 1933) by James Truslow Adams. *School and Society:* "Walter Lippmann and Educational Reconstruction" (September 5, 1942) by Harry D. Gideonse; reprinted by permission of the author. *The Nation:* articles appearing in the issues for September 14, 1927; May 4, 1928; July 5, 1933; July 19, 1933; August 2, 1933; February 27, 1937; November 27, 1937; April 23, 1938; used by permission of the publisher. *Time Magazine:* excerpts from several articles by courtesy of Time, copyright, TIME Inc., 1947 and 1948. *A Free and Responsible Press,* Commission on Freedom of the Press, copyright, 1947, by the University of Chicago Press; used by permission of the publisher. *Vital Speeches:* "Philosophy and United States Foreign Policy" (February 1, 1948) by Walter Lippmann; used by permission of the publisher. *United Nations World:* "Walter Lippmann," May, 1947.

TO BEATRICE

ACKNOWLEDGMENTS

In assembling material for this study the writer solicited the help of many people. Almost all responded favorably. Many extended themselves in his behalf. Those readers who know research at first hand can best appreciate the full measure of gratitude the writer feels. He acknowledges with warmest thanks the indispensable help given by the following:

Professor Erling M. Hunt, sponsor of the study, who gave needed counsel throughout the whole period of the investigation and to whom the writer's debt is very great; Hazel Hammond Albertson, Robert O. Anthony, Dean Bernard Berelson, Dr. Carl Binger, Bruce Bliven, James M. Cain, Frances Davis Cohen, Professor George S. Counts, Professor Ryland W. Crary, Max J. Herzberg, Dr. Alvin Johnson, Dr. Otto Koenig, Dr. Corliss Lamont, Professor Paul F. Lazarsfeld, Dr. David M. Levy, Robert W. Lovett, Daniel Mebane, Charles Merz, Professor Allan Nevins, Nancy Pearson, Professor George Santayana, Richard B. Scandrett, Jr., Professor James T. Shotwell, George Soule, Herbert Bayard Swope, Professor Goodwin B. Watson, Buel F. Weare; the staffs of the Newark and New York public libraries, and the Harvard and Yale libraries; and the numerous persons who, though they gave valued assistance, preferred not to be thanked in print.

This is in no sense an "authorized" study. Mr. Lippmann did, however, graciously answer many questions about his life and work; in every case the footnotes identify his contributions. He gave the writer no personal documents. On the other hand, he did not in any way obstruct the investigation.

CONTENTS

WHY A STUDY OF LIPPMANN?

The surprise election of President Harry S. Truman in 1948 inspired the view that newspapers and their columnists wield far less influence than had always been believed. Some went so far as to say that the election proved the complete independence of the people from the press.

There is no doubt that some dearly held notions were given a much needed shaking-out by the events of November, 1948. But no reputable student of social institutions has suggested that the press, having committed a major blunder, thereby proved its uselessness or its lack of importance. On the contrary, the recent election has spurred critical interest in American journalism. More than ever before it has become a subject of serious study in schools and colleges. The effort to appraise the rôle of the newspaper in a free society has never been more intense.

Leaders in political education have long insisted that regular training in the evaluation of news sources is an urgent phase of civic instruction; that proficiency in appraising the news is a primary skill of citizenship. In an era in which a variety of propagandas contest for the allegiance of the American people, competence in newspaper analysis becomes a national necessity.

Among the important newspaper features are signed columns of opinion. They share, of course, in the sense of authority that newspapers convey. The columnists, with supposed access to unusual sources of information, are regarded by many of their readers as experts. Their statements are popularly quoted to support or attack prevailing views. Readers in large numbers turn to them regularly for guidance on the issues of the day. Column writers are engaged in a kind of continuous adult education on topics of critical importance. As a major opinion-building agency, the columnists merit the most searching investigation.

This study of a leading columnist, Walter Lippmann, is designed to reveal the kind of information that citizens in a democracy should know about the men and women who shape public thinking. Among the questions this study attempts to answer about Mr. Lippmann are the following:

1. What is his background—cultural, educational, economic, political?

2. By what steps did he become a columnist?

3. What are his special qualifications for the position?

4. What have been the dominant influences in his life? What books, personalities, and issues have significantly affected his attitudes?

5. What are the sources of his information? How extensive are his friendships and associations?

6. What are the distinguishing characteristics of his writing?

7. To what pressures is he subject?

8. What are the size and character of his reader-audience?

9. What basic ideas and causes has he advocated?

10. Where has he stood with respect to a series of vital issues that have confronted the American people in recent years?

11. What is the nature of his predictions?

12. To what special interests or prejudices does he appeal?

13. How sound is the information he conveys?

14. How reliable are his interpretations?

15. What is his status among columnists?

For more than three decades Walter Lippmann has held a distinguished place among thinkers on questions of national and international importance. As the author of many books, as newspaper and magazine editor, and as columnist, he has helped to determine the opinions of the American people on many urgent issues. By virtue of his rank in American journalism he is appropriately the subject of special study.

This investigation is primarily concerned with Mr. Lippmann's views on major domestic problems in the years 1932 through 1938. These were years of crisis in American history. In this period most of the important New Deal legislation was proposed and enacted. On all these issues Mr. Lippmann expressed himself in his New York *Herald Tribune* column, "Today and Tomorrow." This study shows exactly where Mr. Lippmann stood in relation to some of the most important of these controversial measures.

The essence of Mr. Lippmann's thinking on foreign affairs, a field in which he has earned special distinction, will be found in Chapter Six "Lippmann As Predictor: National and International Affairs."

Though this study is centered on Mr. Lippmann's newspaper articles for the period mentioned, many references will be found to his books, speeches, and magazine articles. The relation between them and his newspaper columns is, of course, integral; one cannot be studied without reference to the other.

In important respects today's columnists are the counterparts of the great nineteenth-century practitioners of "personal journalism." By this phrase is meant the kind of newspaper writing and editing that conveyed a distinctive, highly individual flavor; it implies the editorial presentation of a personal conception of the news.

The "signed column," as the term is understood today, is essentially a twentieth-century phenomenon. The array of columnists with which present-day newspapers regale their readers was unknown in the Bennett-Greeley-Dana

era of the last century. But in essential respects the columnist has always been with us. The fundamental characteristics of the column are that it constitutes the personal
expression of a known, or at least identifiable writer, presented with some regularity over a period of time.

Isaiah Thomas, Thomas Paine, John Fenno, Philip Fre-
neau, Horace Greeley, James Gordon Bennett, Henry J.
Raymond, and Joseph Pulitzer are the professional ante-
cedents of Westbrook Pegler, Walter Lippmann, Anne
O'Hare McCormick, Dorothy Thompson, and Mark Sullivan. The earlier names include publishers and editors as
well as writers. But to a substantial degree all have exercised the functions of a columnist as here defined; their
discussions of important public matters have either borne
their signatures or been generally attributed to them.

The past century has often been referred to as the "era
of personal journalism." Greeley, Bennett, Raymond,
Dana, and Pulitzer were giants in their day. These writer-
publishers gave a strongly individual quality to their
papers; their passing from the scene was widely interpreted
as the end of personal journalism. But as one of the creative arts, journalism in its nature remains a highly personal
enterprise. Whereas formerly the great editor-publishers
dominated the editorial field, today a group of individual
writers, "columnists," are fulfilling a function resembling
that of the nineteenth-century editors.

One of the most important developments of contemporary journalism is the syndication of newspaper material.
Often thought to be a recent development, it is almost as
old as the press itself. The writings of such major colonial
figures as John Dickinson, Sam Adams, and Thomas Paine,
for example, were very widely reproduced in their own
time. Present-day syndication represents not a new development, but rather the application of twentieth-century mer-
chandising techniques to an old journalistic practice. By
means of syndication a great variety of features is made
available simultaneously to readers all over the country.
This standardization of newspaper fare has been a cause

for concern among certain students who fear the stultifying effects of canned editorials, canned comics, and canned gossip. Whatever the case, there is no doubt that the readership—and presumably the influence—of today's syndicated columnist is vastly greater than that of his nineteenth-century predecessor.

The tradition of personal journalism is nowhere better exemplified than in Walter Lippmann. This study is an attempt to determine his competence for the rôle of opinion molder and an effort to answer the question, "To what degree should readers trust his judgment?" It is hoped, furthermore, that this investigation will point to a way of analyzing the other important builders of public opinion.

INTRODUCTION

It was bound to happen, sooner or later, that an analyst of the news, whether it is pure or adulterated, would one day find himself subjected to a painstaking analysis. If newspapers are properly a subject of careful and objective scrutiny, it follows that columnists, especially those who write critically of domestic and international affairs, should be put under the microscope. This being true, it was natural that Dr. David E. Weingast should have chosen to study what manner of man Walter Lippmann is and how he thinks and why. Certainly Mr. Lippmann can stand scrutiny and critical consideration better than many others who ply the same trade. He may have left a literary trail that is sometimes puzzling. He may even have the appearance at times of being inconsistent. Who has not, who has gone through life with an open mind, constantly seeking for that which is true and good and never hesitating to accept what appears to be the better, through fear of being jeered at for seeming inconsistencies? In any event, the author, before beginning his research, did not have to take numerous shots in anticipation of coming in contact with some noxious disease. Nor, at its conclusion, did it seem advisable thoroughly to disinfect himself.

It is perhaps too easy to ascribe the abundance of the crop of columnists to the aridity of many of the editorial pages of the day. It happens that Walter Lippmann's principal customer is the New York *Herald Tribune* whose editorials are among the fairest and most informative to be found in American newspapers. Others, of greater or lesser standing, have excellent editorial pages and, at the same time, carry an even greater number of columns. Among these, the Washington *Post* and the St. Louis *Post-Dispatch* are notable. It may be that with few exceptions, the modern newspaper, for business or other reasons, does not care to trumpet forth its anathemas with the voice of a Horace Greeley, a Henry Waterman, or a Joseph Pulitzer. Perhaps some of them have found the device of the columnist convenient to say what they themselves, with an ear cocked in the direction of the business office, would not care to say. To be safe, some editors deliberately balance the views of one columnist against the opposing opinions of others. However, one must note that, in many instances, a newspaper may be host to a columnist with a reservation of the right, which is not infrequently exercised, to do a little discreet editing of its own. A newspaper may even decline to print at all a column that might cause some advertiser or social "sacred cow" to moo in protest.

I have thought for some time that there are too many columnists providing such diverse provender as is likely, on occasion, to generate a mental stomachache. Of one thing I am thoroughly persuaded, and that is that some editors gravely fail in their duty to the public in not excluding those columnists who either lack intellectual integrity, or are careless of their facts. They should also be chary of the character assassin, the man who has some personal ax to grind, or some petty revenge to achieve. Sometimes liberties are permitted to be taken that violate good taste or constitute the venting of spite.

So far as Walter Lippmann is concerned, no one can read his column three days a week throughout the years without respecting him, even when one is, at times, disinclined to accept his views. He is seriously doing a serious job. He does not seek to titillate. He does not indulge in jibes, even at one who may have criticized him unfairly.

He is not one to send up a trial balloon and then either trim his sails or go full speed ahead on the basis of what public sentiment seems to be. He is not a sensationalist. He does not write unless he knows what he is writing about. He does not even write for money, although doubtless he is fully conscious of the value of money. He is at all times the serious student and close observer, who tests in the crucible of truth the observations that he proposes to make. He does not regard himself as a seer. He is, in effect, a day-to-day historian. If he errs, as who does not, it is not on account either of dislike or of vindictiveness. He is without cant, and controversy is foreign to a mind that is calm and philosophic and to a soul that is essentially gentle. He gives no impression of a flaming spirit irresistibly pressing him, in spite of his desire to enter the lists with lowered visor and spear in rest to redress a wrong. While striking no personal blows, he does not flinch when blows are leveled at him.

Scholarly, seriously, he presses forward to an eagerly-hoped-for better social order. Yet, at times, he is critical of the measures without which there can be no reasonable hope for betterment. A writer on the New York *World* in the days of its greatness which, necessarily, was before it fell into the clutches of Roy O. Howard, he must have been as personally shocked as his paper was by the judicial murder of Sacco and Vanzetti. And yet, he was able to write an editorial "praising the good intentions of the Lowell Committee after Sacco and Vanzetti were burned...." On the contrary, Heywood Broun, one of the star performers in the *World* orchestra at that same time, abandoned himself to righteous anger at the "good sportsmanship" of a paper that felt that it should "honor the patriotic service" of President A. Lawrence Lowell of Harvard, chairman of the committee that confirmed Governor Fuller's belief in the guilt of these two poor Italian martyrs to the greed of the sordid and the Brahmanism of the Back Bay of Boston. However, one is not to be condemned for saying, in effect, "Well, we have done the best that we could and we must turn our energies in other directions."

As I read the advance proof of this book it seemed to me that Mr. Lippmann probably concurs in the opinion that others of us share, namely, that an unchanging mind is a closed mind and therefore one that is developing sclerosis. It is to Walter Lippmann's credit that, as he explores the world of ideas and ideals, he should modify or even reverse an opinion, although it had been tenaciously held. He might vote for Roosevelt in 1932 on the basis of conditions as they then appeared to him. He might, during the next four years, persuade himself that Roosevelt was leading the country along a dangerous political road. He might therefore conscientiously vote for the minuscule Alf Landon in 1936. The same mind, being an honest one, might well decide, in the greatly changed circumstances that heralded an approaching world-wide conflagration, to vote again for Roosevelt in 1940, and then find himself supporting, in 1944, in the person of Governor Dewey, a candidate with respect to whom he probably had many serious reservations, but whom he had decided to favor for reasons that appeared to him, as to many others, to be valid ones.

A commentator on political and social developments, if he is thoughtful and conscientious, is entitled to respect, even if one may frequently differ with him. Certainly it will do no harm to the traditionalist, the seamless reactionary or the restless liberal to know something of the mental processes of one of the outstanding journalists of his generation. After all, they are the processes of a man who is free and unafraid.

WALTER LIPPMANN

CHAPTER ONE

EARLY LIFE AND CAREER

WALTER LIPPMANN MADE HIS DEBUT AS A COLUMN
writer on September 8, 1931. His entry into the
field was greeted with unconcealed pride by his
new employers, the New York *Herald Tribune*. Having
directed the editorial department of the late New York
World for almost a decade, and having earned a considerable reputation as an author, Lippmann was obviously
regarded by the *Herald Tribune* as a choice accession.
The paper made it clear that he would "write freely upon
such topics as he selects, expressing whatever opinions he
holds." [1]

From the comparative anonymity of newspaper editor,
Lippmann moved to the exposed position of by-lined
writer, whose column appeared four times, later three
times, weekly in papers from coast to coast. His name,
long familiar to the newspaper fraternity and to readers of
serious books, soon became known to a discriminating
newspaper public.

The only child of Jacob and Daisy Baum Lippmann,
Walter was born on Lexington Avenue, between 61st and
62nd Streets, New York City, on September 23, 1889. His
parents, the offspring of German-Jewish immigrants, were
natives of New York City.

Jacob Lippmann was a successful clothing manufac-
turer and real estate broker who retired from business
early in life. His wife, Daisy, an exceedingly attractive

woman and a Hunter College graduate, was the competent manager of a genteel, upper-middle-class home. The third adult in the family was Mrs. Lippmann's mother, a well-to-do, cultured matriarch who had a great fondness for her grandchild, Walter.

The Lippmann household, gracious, well-ordered, and economically secure, was largely focused on the child. An extremely bright, well-mannered youth, Walter was treated as a special kind of person. Never having to cope with brothers and sisters, he was cushioned from the rough-and-tumble experienced by most children. The tiresome chores were done for him by household servants. He took small part in boyhood sports, leaning instead toward reading. Every opportunity was given the precocious youngster for the satisfaction of his great curiosity. Travel to Europe was a regular part of his boyhood experience. Exposed to the best in painting, music, and literature, Walter at an early age had acquired an impressive familiarity with the arts.

From the Lexington Avenue brownstone where he was born, the family moved to an impressive four-story brick home at 121 East 79th Street. They remained there until the boy was thirteen or fourteen, removing then to a handsome stone house at 46 East 80th Street, between Park and Madison. Until his marriage in 1917 he lived at the 80th Street address.

From 1896 to 1906 the boy attended Dr. Julius Sachs' School for Boys, later called The Sachs Collegiate Institute, located at 38 West 59th Street. To this institution, attended chiefly by the sons of well-to-do German-Jewish families, the Jehovah-like Sachs brought a group of first-rate teachers that included Daniel and Frederick Thompson. The latter, eventually to become Professor of History at Amherst, took a great liking to Walter, an outstanding student in history and geography. A quick learner and an avid reader, the handsome boy was usually at the head of his class. It is understandable that he was a favorite of the teachers.

Walter's first piece of published writing appeared in the
Record, a journal for the school's younger students which
for a time he edited. Later he wrote for the school's
monthly, the *Red and Blue.* Among his contributions
were "A Night in a Venetian Palace," in which he related
the uncomfortable experience of sleeping in the suite of
an ancient Italian prince; "A Grave," a sentimental piece
about a child's burial place near the tomb of General
Grant; and "The Apple Woman," a touching description
of a desolate lady who sold apples at the corner of Twenty-
third Street and Fifth Avenue.

Walter also took part in school debates, an annual event
of great importance at Dr. Sachs' institution. In the 1905
contest the team of Sam Arnheim, Carl Binger, and Walter
Lippmann, coached by Arthur Garfield Hays, argued successfully against municipal ownership of street railways
and lighting plants.[2] The following year the same team,
supporting Chinese exclusion, repeated their victory.[3]

A member of a secret club known as Sigma Beta Sigma,
Walter took a full part in the society's rituals. Athletics
had but slight appeal, though he did grow to enjoy tennis.
History, geography, writing, and debating were the fields
in which he excelled. Both in 1904 and 1906 he won the
"Arnold B. Horwitz Prize" for academic achievement.[4]
In 1906 he was graduated under Dr. Otto Koenig, Dr.
Sachs having left the preceding year to become Professor
of Secondary Education at Teachers College, Columbia.

As a boy Lippmann attended Temple Emanu-El, then
located at Fifth Avenue and 43rd Street. Here he received
the conventional religious instruction offered by a reformed congregation. On May 20, 1904, he was confirmed
with his class.

In the fall of 1906 Lippmann entered Harvard, taking
up residence at No. 12 Weld Hall. He occupied a spacious
room and anteroom which were heated by a wood-burning
fireplace, wood being stored in a large closet in his third-
floor suite. His book-lined rooms were among the best
in the house.

Of the twenty-three full or half-year courses listed in the Harvard Archives as comprising Walter's college program, seven were in philosophy, six in French, Latin, and Italian, five in economics, government, and history, three in English and comparative literature, and the remaining two in fine arts and social ethics. For two years he was designated for "Group II" honors, and one year he was included with "Group I" scholars. The former was recognition for "marked excellence" in scholarship, the latter denoted "very high academic distinction." He received both the "John Harvard" scholarship and "Deturs" honors for scholastic excellence, and he was named to Phi Beta Kappa. Though he received the A. B. with his class in 1910, he had completed the degree requirements in three years.

Except for his attempt to make the Weld Dormitory crew in his freshman year and his stint as assistant manager of Harvard's freshman track team, Walter's main interests were in the direction of philosophy, political science, and economics. He managed, in addition, to read extensively in art, poetry, and fiction. Perhaps the dominating intellectual influence of the Harvard years was William James. Although Walter was not a student in any of James' classes, the two met from time to time. In the philosopher's abiding wisdom the eager young scholar found lasting inspiration. George Santayana, too, took notice of the bright youth and came to look upon him and T. S. Eliot as his most promising pupils. Walter, in his fourth year at Harvard, became Santayana's assistant in a course in the History of Philosophy. The visiting English sociologist, Graham Wallas, likewise helped to channelize the young man's thinking and was in a measure responsible for his adherence to Fabian socialism. The strength of the ties between them is attested by Professor Wallas' dedication of his *Great Society* to young Lippmann.

By virtue of his Jewish birth Walter was, of course, ineligible for membership in Harvard's exclusive, caste-ridden clubs. His social life, like that of most undergraduates, was lived outside the rich and snobbish "gold coast." But it was, nevertheless, an expansive, varied experience. He associated with a group of young men who, like himself, were interested in philosophy, art, and political economy; a group who worked in their after-school hours at community centers, including Hale House and Civic Service House. These students, particularly sensitive to the great social stirrings of the times, tended to form their own clubs for the discussion of social and economic problems.

Walter helped to organize the Social Politics Club, a student-faculty group in which a free exchange of views took place. He joined the Harvard Socialist Club, eventually becoming its president. According to the *Harvard Class Album* of 1910, he was also a member of the Debating Club, the Political Club, Circolo Italiano, and the Philosophical Club.

Much of his free time Walter gave to Harvard's literary publications. In one of his early articles, written in 1908 for the *Harvard Illustrated Magazine,* he attacked Barrett Wendell's *The Privileged Classes* for its defense of the rich. For the same publication a year later he also wrote *"Socialism at Harvard."* Here he described the activities of the Harvard Socialist Club, then a year old. He thought it disgraceful that the principles of socialism had barely made an entry into academic quarters. Socialism was, he said, the coming thing. He deplored the innocence of most college students on this supremely important subject. His article was an unequivocal defense of socialism and a strong argument for its inclusion in university programs.

Subsequently in the *Illustrated* he favorably reviewed Hugo Munsterberg's *Psychology and the Teacher* and assailed Price Collier's *England and the English.* Collier had opposed state intervention to relieve the poverty and decay of the British people; Lippmann in his review championed government enterprise to correct economic abuses. In January, 1910 the *Illustrated* published a letter by Lippmann in which he denounced commercialism in football. The injuries and indignities endured by innocent spectators, he argued, were more serious than those which befell the players.

In another *Illustrated* article published in 1910 and called "The Discussion of Socialism" he expressed impatience with the tendency to condemn socialism as something strange and "Marxian." It should, instead, be viewed in its practical, day-to-day significance. "Meet it as a dialectical process in Karl Marx, and it seems terrible and remote. Meet it in the immediate issues of life, and you will find the true sentiment of the nation behind it." Significantly, Lippmann saw a worthwhile "socialism" in conservation, publicly owned utilities, public education, and public sanitation.

For the *Harvard Advocate* he did several book reviews. He also wrote for the *Harvard Monthly,* his name appearing on the board of editors beginning April, 1910. Later that year the *Monthly* published his "In Defense of the Suffragettes" in which he commended the women of England for their aggressive, plain-spoken campaign, adding that "unfortunately, in this world great issues are not won by good manners."

The latter publication also ran his article called "Problem in Imperceptibles" in which he urged a more active participation by students in governmental affairs. He found it "ridiculous for young men to be 'conservative' for it means that they will probably be 'stand-patters' when they grow older."

Subsequently the *Monthly* published articles in which he opposed segregation of students by classes, advocated a more rational organization of Harvard's numerous clubs, and reviewed several plays.

That Walter was regarded by his classmates as a promising young man is epitomized in John Reed's reference to him as "our all-unchallenged chief." Harvardmen still remember the introduction Lippmann was once given by Reed, who presided at Harvard's Western Club. "Once, when Walter Lippmann came to the club as a guest, Reed leaped to his feet, made a sweeping bow, and cried, 'Gen-

tlemen, the future President of the United States!' " [5] If
good looks, fine bearing, modesty, and intelligence were
requisites, young Walter was handsomely equipped for
the job. And the opinion seems to have had wide currency that some day he would achieve it.

The social literature of the early 1900's—Utopian, revolutionary, reformist—had its impact on the Harvard intellectuals. The writings of the great English Fabians—Shaw,
Wells, the Webbs—and the climaxing of a long period of
native social ferment in the muckraking movement agi-
tated great numbers of thinking Americans. A rapidly
growing magazine literature and an outpouring of novels
on social and economic themes dramatized the need for
corrective measures.

Child labor, the exploitation of worker and farmer, the
evil rôle of business in politics, the gouging of the consumer, and corrupt government were exposed to public
view. The Populist and Progressive movements—the political expression of the mounting discontent—held forth the
promise of radical improvement in the lives of the American people. To many it seemed that a bright, new future
was at hand; human values were rising.

Reform had been achieved, some thought, by the mere
act of exposure. To others an uprooting of society itself
seemed necessary before any real betterment could be expected. The Harvard group of intellectuals read, debated,
and, in some cases, acted.

Few members of his group were more earnestly concerned with social problems than Walter Lippmann. In his
work at Hale House in Boston, he came into close touch
with the poorest people in the community. When, on Palm
Sunday of 1908, fire ravaged the nearby town of Chelsea,
he was among the group of Harvard students who labored
for days to help rehabilitate the homeless survivors. From
such experiences came a sharpened interest in the plight
of the depressed classes.

The Harvard group eventually came into association
with Ralph Albertson, an important figure in Boston's

liberal circles. An ordained minister, an advocate of Christian Socialism, Albertson was president of the *Twentieth Century Magazine* and later headed the executive committee that published the *Boston Common;* both periodicals were devoted to social reform.

Walter and his friends were frequent visitors to the Albertson home in Jamaica Plain, outside Boston. There the young intellectuals debated books and the theatre, art and philosophy, and the day's events. There, also, they grew to know and love the Albertson family: Hazel, the beautiful young wife and mother; Phyllis, Chrissie, and Faye, daughters of Ralph by an earlier marriage, and the four children born to Ralph and Hazel.

In 1909 the Albertsons moved to rural West Newbury, Massachusetts, some forty miles north of Boston. The peaceful acres of Chestnut Hill Farm, sloping down to the Merrimac River, had an irresistible appeal to all who saw it, the Harvard boys included. The hospitable Albertsons enjoyed the company of these ardent young spirits who often came out on weekends and holidays. At one time or another the Harvard visitors included, in addition to Walter Lippmann: Carl and Walter Binger, Lee Simonson, Robert Edmond Jones, John Reed, Gerard Henderson, and Felix Frankfurter.

Chestnut Hill had many charms. It was a wonderful place to relax and enjoy the sun, to swim and talk. The vibrant Hazel listened sympathetically, and gave counsel and inspiration. Eager to help her young companions in every way, she created a setting in which they spoke their minds freely. What the Albertson household lacked in organization it provided in human warmth. To the Harvard boys it was the ideal country retreat, peopled with the sweetest souls they knew. Faye Albertson, Ralph's strikingly attractive eldest daughter, became Walter Lippmann's wife in 1917, seven years after he graduated from Harvard.[6]

In his youth Lippmann apparently regarded himself as a good socialist. His membership in the Harvard Socialist Club, his articles in defense of socialism both in college and later, and his acceptance of the secretaryship to the Socialist mayor of Schenectady in 1912 all support this view. But the evidence is strong that socialism to him and to most of his friends meant humanitarianism, social reform, even, perhaps, welfare capitalism. Quite probably it was "socialism of the heart" and "social gospelism." In his own words to the author, he had been a socialist for "only a short time" and "never a Marxist." He had never accepted the idea of the class struggle, he said, but had followed the English Fabian approach of his teacher, Graham Wallas. According to Ernest Sutherland Bates,[7] however, Lippmann at one time held membership in Branch 1, "the most radical of the Socialist groups in New York City." In connection with the mayoralty election of 1913, said Bates, eleven members of Branch 1, Lippmann included, rejected their party's platform and "submitted what was currently called 'a revolutionary left-wing platform' of their own...."

Between the Harvard period and the work in Schenectady, however, the evidence of socialist belief is scanty. In June, 1910, directly upon leaving Harvard, he worked as a reporter for the reformist *Boston Common*. He was commended to the distinguished journalist, Lincoln Steffens, as a bright, promising writer. Steffens engaged him for the staff of *Everybody's Magazine*. Lippmann began by penning an appreciation of William James.[8] Subsequent articles in these same years, 1910 to 1912, had to do with graft in the pension system and the conservation of energy. Nowhere in these articles did he advocate socialism.

On January 1, 1912, Lippmann became executive secretary to the Rev. George R. Lunn, Socialist mayor of Schenectady. The victory of Mr. Lunn had aroused high hopes among Socialists everywhere. To many it seemed that the Socialist millennium had arrived. In an article for *The Masses* (not to be confused with the present-day *New Masses*), a publication that opposed direct action and favored parliamentary reforms, Lippmann told of the many inquiries that came in from Socialists asking for guidance. He expressed his conviction that a bold Socialist program should be undertaken. "Playing safe ... may be very dangerous in the long run. For it confuses Socialism with reform politics and tends to impregnate the movement with half baked people who don't understand Socialism."

The trafficking, the pressures, the tensions that characterize practical politics were not wanting at Schenectady. Young Lippmann did not relish standing in the midst of it all and after only four months in office he resigned his job. He had come to feel, apparently, that the administration was trying to execute a program that the people of Schenectady hadn't even begun to understand. A huge program of education would be required to make clear the purposes of a Socialist regime. The "hinterland," he complained, hadn't been cultivated. As a result, the administration had been forced to mold its program along the conventional lines to which the community had grown accustomed. He even became contemptuous of that "large wing" of the Socialist Party that had become the slave of "obvious success," the winning of elections. There was a great difference, he said, between "voting the Socialist ticket and understanding Socialism." [9]

Lippmann forecast his own rôle in life by agreeing with H. G. Wells as to the futility of trying to "fix up" human affairs; it would be much better to devote himself to the "'development of that needed intellectual life without which all ... shallow attempts at fixing up are futile.'" [10] He confessed that "there was something monotonously trivial and irrelevant about our reformist enthusiasm...." [11] The grubby work of day-to-day politics had become distasteful to Lippmann. He was eager, moreover, to get down on paper some ideas he had been mulling over for a book—*Preface to Politics*.

This, his first volume, looked with a certain tolerance at socialism,[12] though it was far from Marxist in its orientation. His second work, *Drift and Mastery*, published in

1914, found Marx a poor prophet and the socialist movement sterile.[13] Lippmann's developing hostility to socialism was climaxed in his most important volume, appearing in 1937 under the title *Good Society*.[14] Here he brought to bear his extensive study of economics and political science to refute completely the socialist thesis. In this work Lippmann reduced the whole complex of socialist dogma to the mere transfer of title deeds from private individuals to the community as a whole. He stripped socialism of its ideological justification, maintaining that the evils besetting society would in no way be relieved by vesting ownership in the state.

Lippmann's alienation from socialism is thus seen to be complete. But even when the union was closest, his participation was somehow detached in character; it was, predominantly, support for social reformism rather than social revolution. The subtle influences of a lifetime of middle-class comfort and a growing ambition to achieve wealth and fame undoubtedly helped to refashion Lippmann's convictions. Essentially conservative by tradition and personal predilection, he had dabbled briefly and lightly in socialism. Within three years of his leaving Harvard there was scarcely a trace of active interest left. He has, of course, continued to be concerned for the economically deprived. While his program for relieving social distress has itself gone through a metamorphosis, his interest, judged by his writing, has remained acute.

In 1913 Lippmann was invited by Herbert Croly to become associated with him in the production of a new journal of opinion. Croly, author of *The Promise of American Life*, had secured the backing of the financier, Willard Straight, for the project.[15] Ultimately called the *New Republic*, the magazine was designed to advocate progressive principles. As Croly saw its purpose, it was "less to inform or entertain readers than to start little insurrections in the realm of their convictions." [16] Croly engaged the interest of Philip Littell, Walter E. Weyl, Francis Hackett,

and Charles Rudyard in addition to Lippmann. Latez
Alvin Johnson and Charles Merz joined the board of
editors. On November 7, 1914, the *New Republic* made
its first appearance. Lippmann's contribution to that issue
consisted of a review of H. G. Wells' *The Wife of Sir
Isaac Harman.*

At weekly conferences presided over by Croly, decisions
were hammered out on the views to be elaborated by
the editors. Started as a champion of the policies of Theodore Roosevelt, the paper began early to support Woodrow
Wilson. It came finally to be regarded as the voice of the
Administration, though Lippmann has offered testimony
that there was no calculated effort to harmonize the views
of the paper with those of the President.

Our relations with Wilson were never personal. I don't think
Croly ever saw Wilson when he was President; in the winter
of 1916 I had two or three interviews, such as any journalist
has with the President. Croly and I did begin to see something
of Colonel House. It was a curious relationship. Wilson was
preparing to run for his second term; his main problem was
the management of American neutrality. We discussed the
problem perhaps once a fortnight with Colonel House. He
never told us what the President was going to do. We never
knew anything that hadn't appeared in the newspapers. In our
own minds we followed the logic of the situation as we saw it.
Partly by coincidence, partly by a certain parallelism of reason-
ing, certainly by no direct inspiration either from the President
or Colonel House, *The New Republic* often advocated policies
which Wilson pursued. The legend grew that *The New Republic* was Wilson's organ.... The paper was never the organ
of the Wilson administration. We never knew any secrets, we
never had a request to publish or not to publish anything,
and we were not in a confidential relationship.[17]

Yet many who were on the scene at the time insist that
Woodrow Wilson and Walter Lippmann were much
closer than Lippmann admitted. Some careful observers
maintain that Wilson used Lippmann's ideas and even,
occasionally, his language. It is possible, of course, that

Colonel House was the primary means of contact between the two men.

When the United States entered the war in 1917, Secretary of War Newton D. Baker, with whom Lippmann had been very friendly, invited the young writer to come to Washington. There Lippmann was appointed an assistant to Mr. Baker to handle labor problems connected with war production. In conversation with the author, Mr. Lippmann said that much of the negotiation was carried on with Samuel Gompers, spokesman for the American Federation of Labor. Lippmann represented the army on numerous committees, including one on which Franklin D. Roosevelt, then an assistant secretary, represented the Navy. This work continued through the summer of 1917.

Toward the end of the summer President Wilson and Colonel House began to feel that systematic preparations for the peace conference should be undertaken. They projected the idea of a research body whose task it would be to marshal data of a geographic, ethnic, and political character for our government's use at the end of the war. The President of the College of the City of New York, Dr. Sidney E. Mezes, who was also House's brother-in-law, was named to head the organization. Lippmann, as executive secretary, Professor James T. Shotwell, historian and editor, and the distinguished lawyer, David Hunter Miller, formed the nucleus of the group. There was no provision for this type of activity in the State Department or elsewhere. The committee's expenses, Mr. Lippmann told the author, were therefore met out of private funds available to President Wilson.

The organization acted in complete secrecy, lest the impression go out that our government was considering a capitulation. To cloak the committee's activities Professor Shotwell suggested it be called by the cryptic title "The Inquiry." [18] The group invited Dr. Isaiah Bowman, director of the American Geographical Society, to become associated with the work. "... while the organization remained under the titular chairmanship of Dr. Mezes, as time went on the burden of the day fell more and more upon Dr. Bowman, who was both Chief Territorial Expert and Executive Officer." [19]

The earliest meetings were held at the New York Public Library. Because of the lack of space and the fear of attracting public notice to their activities, the organization moved to the building of the American Geographical Society, Broadway at 156th Street. Here the members had at their disposal the Society's elaborate facilities for conducting their studies. According to Mr. Lippmann, approximately 150 scholars and specialists assembled to collect facts for eventual use at the peace conference.

In November, 1917, the Bolsheviks came into power in Russia. Rebuffed in their efforts to obtain an armistice, they published the archives of the Czar's Foreign Office, thereby making known to the world the territorial ambitions of the Allied governments. House urged upon Wilson a strong declaration designed to neutralize the damaging effects of the Bolshevik revelations, and to galvanize liberal and labor groups here and abroad into more vigorous support of the war. Thereupon Wilson ordered The Inquiry to write a suitable statement. They prepared eight memoranda, "the territorial sections of the Fourteen Points." [20] The Inquiry's document, with some additions, was given by the President to Congress and the world in January, 1918.

Growing restless with the work in New York, Lippmann accepted a commission to do political propaganda work abroad. He was also under instructions by the State Department to establish liaison with the British propaganda division under Lord Northcliffe and Sir Campbell Stuart. From July to November, 1918, Lippmann, an Army captain, was part of a six-man unit that directed a barrage of propaganda across the German lines. Utilizing Wilson's statements, the group exhorted the Germans to recognize the hopelessness of the struggle and surrender. The Army paper, *Stars and Stripes,* testified to the effectiveness of the unit's work: "Of the thousands of prisoners who passed through the examining cage of a single American corps during the first fortnight of the Meuse-Argonne campaign, it was found, upon examination, that one out of every three had our propaganda in his pocket. And this despite the fact that the German high command had decreed it a treasonable offense for any soldier so much as to have the accursed stuff in his possession." [21]

Following the collapse of Bulgaria in September, 1918, Lippmann left the Meuse-Argonne front for Paris where he was attached to Colonel House's staff. The Germans having agreed to surrender on the basis of the Fourteen Points, House had to obtain the approval of Lloyd George and Orlando to a capitulation on those terms. The British and Italian leaders wanted to know what Wilson's declaration meant. To Lippmann went the task of preparing an explanation. Writing all night, he completed thirteen memoranda, Frank Cobb of the *World* supplying the fourteenth. The memoranda were cabled to Wilson, who gave them his approval. [22]

President Wilson's decision to go to the Paris Peace Conference seemed to Lippmann an unfortunate mistake. He felt that the President's commitments were so final that compromise and adjustment would be impossible with Wilson heading his own delegation. Lippmann was also distressed by big-power intervention against the newly created Soviet Union. "I tried in vain," he said, "to remind Wilson of the incongruity of the situation. I pointed out that by participating in this war during the era of pacification we were bound to cancel out the effectiveness of the peace treaty we were drafting." In dismay Lippmann left the Peace Conference. [23]

After his return to the United States Lippmann resumed work on the *New Republic* for a brief period. He resigned in order to finish his book, *Public Opinion,* and shortly thereafter he was invited by Herbert Bayard Swope, executive editor of the New York *World,* to join his publication. For two years Lippmann wrote editorials. Following Editor Frank Cobb's death in 1923, Lippmann was given charge of the *World's* editorial page. From 1929 until the paper ceased to publish in 1931, Lippmann, with the same general duties, bore the title Editor.

Lippmann's departure from the *New Republic* was a grave disappointment to Croly, who believed that the magazine's mission transcended in importance any individual's personal fortune. For his close associate to take a more lucrative position seemed to Croly unpardonable opportunism.

The *World* offered Lippmann a forum of vastly greater dimensions than the *New Republic*. His editorials, sedate and scholarly, were strongly for the public welfare and against the privilege hunters. According to journalist-historian Allan Nevins, the main ideas of the paper under Cobb, internationalism, more democracy, a stronger stand against plutocratic tendencies and special privilege, were dominant principles under Lippmann, too. In the words of one observer, "The distinguishing quality of the *World* was its editorial page. Lippmann was its presiding genius."

As Lippmann himself pointed out later, he devoted much of his time on the *World* to "fighting the Harding, Coolidge, and Hoover Administrations." [24] In the period of Lippmann's editorship the paper did a vigorous job of exposing the Jess Smith-Harry Daugherty scandals that disgraced the Harding Presidency, battled the Ku Klux Klan, forced improvements in the conditions under which the miners of West Virginia had been living, and gave strong support to Al Smith's Presidential candidacy. [25] The paper was also credited with the abolition of contract prison labor in Alabama. [26] Nevins observed that "The main battle of the *World* in these years was for an international spirit—for the World Court, for lower tariffs and more world trade, for co-operation with the League, and in general for salvaging as much of the Wilsonian program as possible. A secondary battle was against Mellonism and the Mellon financial policies." [27]

The *World,* while it held the Sacco-Vanzetti decision unjust, felt that the commission that reviewed the case and sustained the judgment should nevertheless be thanked. This incensed Heywood Broun who was reminded of the annual football game between Yale and Harvard. At the end of the contest, Broun observed, all strife and rancor ceased. "This is a practice known as sportsmanship.... But I am shocked to find those who would extend these under-graduate rites to conflicts more serious and weighty. Sacco and Vanzetti being dead, there are liberal journals who would have us all forget and love our neighbors without discrimination." Broun was outraged by the *World's* desire to "honor the patriotic service" of Harvard President Ab-bott Lawrence Lowell, head of the committee that con-firmed Governor Fuller's belief in the guilt of Sacco and Vanzetti.[28] Broun also charged that the *World* had fre-quently "been able to take two, three, or even four dif-ferent stands with precisely the same material in hand." He thought the paper had neither courage nor tenacity and was excessively fearful of offending pressure groups.[29]

James M. Cain, the novelist, who was associated with Mr. Lippmann on the *World's* editorial staff for almost a decade, thought that the paper's difficulties stemmed from the gentlemanliness of Ralph Pulitzer, the publisher. Un-like Joseph, the energetic founder of the *World,* son Ralph had no stomach for the rough and tumble of newspaper work. Moreover, said Cain, he tended to hire gentlemen—Walter Lippmann, for example—to run his paper. Cain, too, took exception to Lippmann's publishing a piece "praising the good intentions of the Lowell committee after Sacco and Vanzetti were burned...."

Lippmann, Cain said, "is not faint-hearted and he is not an editor. Nobody who ever tried to buck him on any issue whatever could have any doubts about his spirit: he will not trim, he will not back down, and he will not compromise.... And nobody who watched his boredom with the job of getting out his page... could have supposed that he was an editor. He had no interest in editing, and it is not surprising that his page often showed it."[30]

Cain has since emphasized that one of Lippmann's distinguishing characteristics was a "courtesy far finer than is commonly encountered on newspapers." Toward his editorial staff Lippmann took the position that a man should write only for an idea in which he believed. Lippmann's value, Cain added,

was to explore new lines of thought, rather than take solid positions of value to his paper. He was, and is, I think, rather indifferent to what is good for his paper, not from temperamental unreasonableness ... but from an inability to gear his mind to such special considerations. He is considerably bigger than any paper likely to hire him ... and thinks in large terms, quite divorced from momentary exigencies the front office may be worrying about. Indeed, he may be thinking in terms quite divorced from what the American people are worrying about, which occasionally gives his work an extremely far-fetched quality. And yet, when most of us were worrying about cars ... he was proclaiming the impending collapse of Europe.[31]

Allan Nevins maintained that Lippmann was an able, conscientious editor who held a good editorial conference; included on his staff were Charles Merz, later to become editor of the *New York Times,* Nevins, and Cain. In a memorandum to the author, Nevins said Lippmann "read editorials carefully and lifted the page to a distinctly higher intellectual level than Cobb." Lippmann kept the *World* "one of the citadels of American liberalism. It was liberal in a fashion that showed a little of Croly's influence, a little more of Wallas's and a great deal of Frank Cobb's but that represented, most of all, Mr. Lippmann's own attitude." [32]

Cobb had the faculty of hitting hard, of putting ideas strongly and clearly. He went after the forces of evil "with a meat-axe." Lippmann, on the other hand, did not see issues in terms of black or white. He was more deliberate, judicious, and subtle in his analyses. Consequently, while he appealed to the better-educated readers, he often confused people of simple minds.

Many reasons have been given for the *World's* disappearance. According to one witness the paper had too diverse an appeal, with an editorial page designed for intellectuals and a comic section that attracted morons. Another close observer asserted that "while the *Times* and *Herald Tribune* constantly took away the better-class readers from the *World* by printing more news, the *Daily News* and *Mirror* steadily took away the poorer-class readers by printing more sensationalism. The *World* was caught between two competitive millstones." [33] In 1931 the paper was sold to the Scripps-Howard interests, who merged it with the *Telegram*.

At forty-two Walter Lippmann stood ready for new undertakings. By background, training, and ability he was supremely well equipped for a variety of callings: diplomacy, scholarship, letters—or journalism. While his friends debated which would claim him, he received an invitation from Mr. and Mrs. Ogden Reid to write an independent column for the New York *Herald Tribune*. Many of his admirers were astonished by his acceptance. They found it incongruous that a liberal journalist should be published by an arch-Republican paper. One or the other would be converted. Lippmann had embarked on the most controversial phase of his career.

CHAPTER TWO

LIPPMANN AS COLUMNIST

SINCE SEPTEMBER, 1931, WHEN HE BEGAN WRITING HIS column, "Today and Tomorrow"—referred to in the trade as "T. and T."—for the New York *Herald Tribune,* Lippmann's articles have been widely syndicated. At the present time his column is published in 140 newspapers, including every important city in the country, with few exceptions. In most of these cities the leading paper subscribes to his column. He also appears in nine Canadian, and seventeen Latin American publications, as well as in Australian, Greek, Japanese, and Hawaiian papers.

The *Herald Tribune* and *Washington Post* regularly publish Lippmann's column with the standard heading and topical subheading he provides. In these papers, also, the article appears in a fixed position on the page. Many of the other papers vary this procedure, supplying their own titles and deleting or omitting pretty much at will.

Unlike many syndicated features, Lippmann's column is sold alone, rather than in a "parcel" of assorted items. Papers buy his articles on a yearly contract, the price they pay depending on such factors as their circulation, their importance, and the competition they face. Syndicates as a rule charge what the traffic will bear.

Neither the *Herald Tribune* nor the Syndicate has censored or pressured Walter Lippmann; both have adhered to the terms of the original understanding by which Lippmann was given full freedom of expression.

Shunning the trivial, the personal, and the seemingly transitory items, Lippmann has addressed himself to major national and international developments. His essays constitute thoughtful and serious commentary on the basic questions that have faced the nation and the world in a period of growing crisis.[1]

To his task as interpreter of public affairs Lippmann has brought great intelligence and an imposing background of study in history, economics, government, and philosophy. His spacious study overflows with books on a great variety of subjects. Reference books, encyclopedias, atlases abound; London papers handily stacked, a globe at his elbow, a shortwave radio within reach; these are his primary tools.[2] He is not, according to a close friend, "a Germanic scholar. He doesn't read shelves of books on a subject; he is something far more important: a selective scholar.... He has an extraordinarily well-informed mind which covers a great range of subjects. He has a tremendous knowledge of important relationships and developments in many different fields. He is not the supreme scholar in any one tiny segment of learning."

Allan Nevins noted that one year, back in the New York *World* days, he borrowed library books for Walter Lippmann, then his colleague. Lippmann's borrowings that winter "were fairly numerous but the most striking fact about them...would have been their catholicity. One group of books referred to the growth of the law, the reform of court procedure in England and America, and the processes by which constitutions and codes are altered without formal amendment. Another group, if I remember aright, dealt with international affairs. But the largest group was of books bearing on philosophy, religion and ethics." [3] It is difficult to conceive of a newspaperman persisting more earnestly in the task of keeping himself informed.

Lippmann's writing reflects a familiarity with the great literature of all periods. His discussions of contemporary economic and social problems are fortified with frequent

citations from the abstract and technical reports issuing
from official sources. The evidence of painstaking gather-
ing and collating of facts is indisputable. He does his own
research, being assisted only by a reference librarian. To
a degree perhaps unique among the working press, Lippmann documents his interpretations by reference to authorities, many well known, some obscure. The accoutre-
ments of serious scholarship are ever present in his writing.

Lippmann works on his column each morning from
nine to twelve. His self-discipline in this respect is a source
of unending comment among those who know him. Af-
ternoons are spent in reading, physical exercise, and social
activity. For a little over ten years he has lived in Washington, D. C., where he occupies a handsome house in exclusive Georgetown. According to one friend, Lippmann
made the move "when the capital was transferred" from
New York. He feels, apparently, that residence in Washington is indispensable to doing his job satisfactorily. He
is a member of the most important clubs in both cities. In
Washington he belongs to the Cosmos, Army and Navy,
Metropolitan, and Army-Navy Country Clubs; in New
York City to the Century, Harvard, Coffee House, and
River Clubs. It would be difficult to name a brace of clubs
anywhere in the country that attracts a more distinguished
or celebrated following. Washington's Cosmos Club, for
example, includes the leaders among the world's diplomats.
The Century Club in Manhattan has for over a hundred
years numbered among its restricted membership nation-
ally important figures in the arts and professions. Lippmann's social coverage is very extensive, embracing top
personalities among government officials, the press, the international diplomatic corps, the military set, and the
world of business.

Among Lippmann's intimates in earlier years were Harold J. Laski and Felix Frankfurter. Laski's *Political
Thought in England from Locke to Bentham,* published
in 1920, contains an affectionate dedication to Walter
Lippmann. For almost a decade before Dwight Morrow's

death in 1931, he and the columnist were warm friends. Morrow's ripe, inventive intellect, and Lippmann's eager, perceptive mind were well matched; in this association ideas germinated and flourished. The Morrows shunned the Newport-Palm Beach atmosphere. Their friends—and Lippmann's—were distinguished by their achievements rather than by the mere possession of wealth. Thomas Lamont and Russell C. Leffingwell, leaders in the House of Morgan, as well as Judge Learned Hand moved in this group. With Mr. Lamont, especially, Lippmann became close friends. Until the columnist moved to Washington the two saw each other frequently.

Lippmann is known to have been on very friendly terms with Cordell Hull until they broke over French policy at the time of the invasion of North Africa, and with former Under-Secretary of State Sumner Welles. On a given evening at the Lippmann home have appeared the French journalist, Pertinax; the French Ambassador, Henri Bonnet, and former Assistant Secretary of State Spruille Braden.

Lippmann's associations with the mighty have been the subject of much acid comment. The feeling persists among some of his early acquaintances that he belongs on the barricades; that he should have become the intellectual leader of America's masses. Some have thought him a climber who, with much to offer on his own, has nevertheless gratefully and humbly accepted recognition by the powerful. Others, while conceding higher motives, believe that he was intellectually seduced by his important hosts, whose apologist he has unwittingly become. Still others regard him as a master craftsman in his field who has built and continues to nourish priceless contacts among the great and important—the policy makers in this and other countries. There is strong evidence to sustain the last view.

To many acquaintances Lippmann appears to be an introvert who is seldom expansive. But in the society of the people he likes he is regarded as "regular," as one who enjoys a good evening-out for its own sake, who freely participates in the give-and-take of a social occasion. He is a highly engaging person, soft-spoken, unfailingly courteous, and thoroughly charming.

Lippmann is, undoubtedly, a respecter of persons. But that he depends on "persons" for the raw material of his columns. Numerous individuals who know him well have testified to his constant search for ideas. Some of his friends feel that if they say something clever or profound in his presence, it is likely to appear in his column—without benefit of a credit line. He has been quoted as saying that he recognizes "no copyright on ideas." His powerful friends and acquaintances are a fertile source of information. A conscientious researcher, he could hardly be expected to ignore such productive fountainheads of intelligence. It must also be recognized that Mr. Lippmann's attention is sought by many of the important people he sees. Diplomats, army leaders, government officials, and the various other celebrities and near-celebrities he encounters are eager for his friendly notice as a matter of good public relations. His stature in the world of journalism makes him a person to be cultivated. Not to be overlooked in any evaluation of Lippmann's social life is the understandable envy of those who "knew him when...."

An obvious deficiency in his social program is his failure to associate extensively with lower-than-top-strata personalities. He appears to be most comfortable in the society of leaders in politics, business, and the arts, and does not seem to have developed friendships with labor or farm people, or with the leaders of mass movements. His contact with rank-and-file groups is indirect. Undoubtedly his value as an interpreter of the world scene would be enhanced if his associations were better balanced.

It is reasonable to assume that Lippmann is exposed to much of the gossip and intrigue that permeate the atmosphere of any national capital. His articles, however, are devoid of the personal chit-chat that fills many of the columns originating in Washington. The information he acquires in his social life he incorporates in his exposition of issues. His essays rarely deal with personalities. Usually he mentions individuals in relation to broad and important questions, infrequently in any other connection.

Writing in a small, fine hand which is almost illegible, Lippmann turns out an essay ranging from 700 to 1,200 words in a morning. A singular characteristic of his writing, true in the early *New Republic* days as well as now, is that Lippmann's original manuscript is "clean copy," almost entirely free of corrections.

Lippmann's orderly prose is the work of a disciplined, informed mind. He long ago established himself as a technician skilled in his craft, with a notable ability to translate abstract and complex issues into understandable English. One of his early columns on international exchange, "Payments in Kind"; [4] his chapter on trade unionism in *Drift and Mastery;* [5] his discussion called "Huey Long's Radio Speech"; [6] and his analysis of the principles of self-determination contained in *U.S. War Aims* [7] are typical of Lippmann's style. There, as in most of his writing, modest but compelling conclusions follow carefully constructed argument.

James M. Cain has spoken of Lippmann's "passion for fine work." As editor of the *World* Lippmann spent many weary hours translating what he called the "flat-wheel sentences" of ungifted colleagues into what he regarded as English. Lippmann's "syntactical fussiness is still visible in his writings, and could be emulated by other writers for newspapers." [8]

Barbarisms and improprieties are rarely found in Lippmanns writing. He has warned against generalizing from an inadequate sample,[9] thinking in terms of stereotypes,[10] and accepting "sequence or parallelism as equivalent to cause and effect." [11] He has exposed the meaninglessness of such terms as the "French mind, the militarist mind, the bolshevik mind...." [12]

By and large Lippmann's writings are free from the weaknesses against which he has cautioned. The exceptions are relatively few in number. In one column, for example, he found with perhaps questionable certainty that "Americans do not take public relief till they absolutely must...." [13] Similarly, he pointed to the "preference of the English-speaking peoples for crossing bridges when you [sic] come to them...." [14] In paying tribute to the authors of *The Federalist*, Lippmann declared categorically that there is no one alive at the present time who "believes in general principles as did the authors of those essays.... These men possessed an intellectual clarity that we have wholly lost." [15] Elsewhere in the same discussion Lippmann reached the curious conclusion that "...well down into the nineteenth century, the mass of men were, as Gladstone put it, passive. They had prejudices, but they were stable prejudices." [16] These dubious generalizations, it should be emphasized again, represent Lippmann's deviations and not his norm.

Through all of Lippmann's writing runs a strong quality of earnestness. This was true of the opinionated *Preface to Politics* and *Drift and Mastery*, with which he began his professional career; it is true today. The later writing, understandably, conveys a sense of sobriety and a maturity lacking in the earlier works. But characteristic of all his writing is the sincerity of a honest mind revealing itself. With great candor he remarked in the Introduction to *Good Society*,

For more than twenty years I have found myself writing about critical events with no better guide to their meaning than the hastily improvised generalizations of a rather bewildered man. Many a time I have wanted to stop talking and find out what I really believed. For I should have liked to achieve again the untroubled certainty and assured consistency which are vouchsafed to those who can wholeheartedly commit themselves to some one of the many schools of doctrine. But I was not able to find in any of the schools a working philosophy in which I could confidently come to rest.[17]

Lippmann scorns the rôle of prophet. His writing is restrained, judicious, and reasonable, and almost never alarmist. Characteristic of his caution was his discussion of French policy toward Spain in the early months of the civil war when he declared, "It may mark, I think, a decisive turn provided it is resolutely pursued." [18] On another occasion he commented on "... the return of prosperity, which, barring unforeseen contingencies in the outer world, seems now to be assured...." [19] *Time* magazine, usually friendly, called attention to this circuitous statement in a Lippmann column discussing the Berlin blockade in 1948: "It was never possible, we must I believe suppose, that we could induce the Russians to lift the blockade unless..." On this occasion, noted *Time*, Lippmann "got his claws tangled with his beak." [20]

Only rarely does Lippmann importune or seek to make converts. His writing is free of any missionary spirit. Because he is wedded to no party or faction he is free to criticize all groups and all policies. To an analyzer of public events there are undoubted advantages in holding such a position.

Bursts of wrath, ill-considered predictions, and boasts about his correct guesses are alien to Lippmann's temperament. In serene confidence he makes his observations; in consistent good taste he ignores his victories. Controversies are shunned; he rarely takes public notice of attacks on him, though some have been bitter. A case in point was Lippmann's dispute with Frank R. Kent of the *Baltimore Sun* on the question of whether the relief rolls were a satisfactory index of the severity of the depression. Kent had declared that the "failure" of the New Deal pained Lippmann because he was an early supporter. Kent continued by saying, "When things seem particularly sick in Washington, Mr. Lippmann deplores the confusion and then goes cosmic, becomes so pontifical and profound that no one can follow him." [21] Lippmann's answer was, "on the question at issue ... there is nothing further to say at the moment, and I shall not reply to Mr. Kent's personal comments because all that would come of that would be that I might lose a good friend in trying to win an unimportant argument." [22] Reference has been made in Chapter I to his amiable feelings toward the Lowell committee in the Sacco-Vanzetti affair.

The recommendation of the Commission on Freedom of the Press that "members of the press engage in vigorous mutual criticism" [23] evoked no enthusiasm from Lippmann. He belongs, according to *Time,* to the "country-club school of newspapering, in which club members do not discuss each other aloud." Lippmann declared that newspapermen, after all, do " 'have to see each other' " and " 'work together.' " His experience with mutual criticism, he concluded, was that " 'the hard feelings it causes are out of all proportion to the public benefits it causes.' " [24]

Lippmann is not in the fight. He wears no battle scars because he is an observer rather than a participant in the struggle. He has elected a position that is detached and somewhat remote. In remarkable degree he seems to have followed the advice he once gave to a Columbia University graduating class when he urged that scholars withdraw from the chaotic world and devote themselves to their intellectual pursuits.

... I doubt whether the student can do a greater work for his nation in this great moment of its history than to detach himself from its preoccupations, refusing to let himself be absorbed by distractions about which, as a scholar, he can do almost nothing. For this is not the last crisis in human affairs. The world will go on somehow, and more crises will follow. It will go on best, however, if among us there are men who have stood apart, who refused to be anxious or too much concerned, who were cool and inquiring, and had their eyes on a longer past and a longer future. [25]

Lippmann does not direct his column to the masses. The level of his writing and the ideas he advocates appeal to a minority of newspaper readers. According to a well-known scale for measuring the difficulty of reading matter, Lippmann's columns are rated as "fairly difficult." [26]

This yardstick reveals that 40 per cent of American adults are capable of understanding his columns, and 24 per cent constitute a "typical" reader-audience. Lippmann's writing was proved to be on the level of that found in "quality" magazines.

The American newspapers subscribing to Lippmann's column have a total circulation of about 12,000,000. To this must be added Canadian and Latin American circulation equalling 1,350,000. This gives a combined total for continental America of well over 13,000,000.[27]

Almost all the papers that publish Lippmann's column express a definite political belief. Circulations according to the self-designated preferences of the papers are as follows:

Democratic	617,000
Independent Democratic	2,807,000
Independent	4,542,000
Independent Republican	1,962,000
Republican	1,041,000
Undesignated	1,000,000
	11,969,000

What part of this potential audience actually reads Lippmann's column? It is not possible to say with certainty, but some estimates have been made, based on approved sampling techniques.

A *Fortune* Survey found that 35.8 per cent of newspaper readers actually read syndicated columnists.[28] Applied to Walter Lippmann, this percentage would suggest a readership in the United States of 4,296,000. It is known, however, that 39 per cent of American newspapers publish four or more political columnists, in addition to various others.[29] The *Fortune* figures give *total* column-readership rather than the readership for a particular column. Divided by three, possibly, the *Fortune* totals would come close to indicating Lippmann's actual reader-following. This would give him a readership of around one-and-a-half million.

Since a large proportion of newspapers are read by more than one person, this figure represents minimum readership.

In its 1940 study *Fortune* ranked Lippmann fourth in popularity among syndicated columnists. The readership of Walter Winchell, Dorothy Thompson, and Boake Carter exceeded his. Lippmann surpassed Heywood Broun, Westbrook Pegler, and David Lawrence.

Among "prosperous" readers Miss Thompson was the favorite, Lippmann second. Among low-income readers Walter Winchell was first, Lippmann last in popularity. Lippmann's readers, according to the same study, were "potential Republicans." [30]

According to the findings of the *Continuing Study of Newspaper Reading* in its 1946 analysis of the six best-read columnists, Walter Lippmann ranked fifth as the favorite columnist of men readers, and sixth with women readers. Among men readers he was outranked by Drew Pearson, Westbrook Pegler, George E. Sokolsky, and Paul Mallon. David Lawrence trailed Lippmann. Women readers favored Eleanor Roosevelt, Sokolsky, Miss Thompson, Pegler, and Pearson over Lippmann. [31]

The rewards of writing, in Walter Lippmann's case, have been prodigious. He is regarded as the highest-paid serious writer in the business. For his column he receives a substantial salary and commission, and a contract that guarantees him generous time for travel and vacationing. He is believed by friends to be a thrifty person who has made good investments. *Time* [32] on one occasion said that his yearly income was $54,329. Others have placed the figure very much higher. Because of his dislike of public speaking he has spurned lucrative opportunities to talk on the radio and on the lecture platform.

What has Lippmann told his readers on some of the great economic and social problems that have plagued the American people in recent years? Subsequent chapters will give attention to this question.

CHAPTER THREE

LIPPMANN'S ECONOMIC VIEWS

PERHAPS THE KEY TO WALTER LIPPMANN'S ECONOMIC views is to be found in a 1934 column he wrote regarding Professor Rexford Guy Tugwell's fitness for the post of Under-Secretary of Agriculture. Defending the appointment, the columnist declared that Tugwell, though he might once have been a Fabian Socialist, had steadily grown more conservative under the pressure of realities. Those who abandoned the doctrine of socialism, Lippmann added, became objects of suspicion to those who remained loyal. The ex-socialists were, understandably, denounced as "time servers" and "straddlers." Some of them were properly condemned. "But many of them are honest men who won't deny facts when they see them, even if the facts cannot be squared with their previous opinions." [1]

In effect Lippmann was here justifying his own abandonment of left-wing principles in favor of more conservative views. That Lippmann has actually travelled a long road, ideologically speaking, is abundantly clear from his writing. His own words on the subject to the author are unequivocal: "I was once a socialist myself."

The point is made in Chapter I that Walter Lippmann's "socialism" had a tenuous quality; that it was shortlived and does not seem to have represented a deep and abiding conviction. To belabor him, therefore, as a deserter from the Marxist camp is to attribute to him an affiliation that scarcely existed in fact.[2]

But if Walter Lippmann was never an orthodox Marxist, it is none the less true that he was a vigorous protagonist of social reform. His first book, *Preface to Politics,*
a critique of modern industrial society, contained a justification of syndicalism. In this indictment of the existing
order, Lippmann detailed the objections of the syndicalists
to capitalism: our industrial system thwarted basic human
impulses; it was a force that condemned its many victims
to poverty and suffering; it meant the "ruthless denial of
life to millions of men." [3]

In his second work, *Drift and Mastery,* he discussed
some implications of modern industry, to which he referred as "the great fact in our lives, blackening our cities,
fed with the lives of children, a tyrant over men and
women...." He spoke of the long-standing desire of reformers to supplant the system of private ownership with
something designed to promote a greater fulfillment of
human aspirations. [4] In articles written for the *New Republic* he continued his assault on social evils and underscored his demand for remedial measures. [5]

In the early New Deal period Lippmann wrote many
times in favor of government intervention to secure the
economic well-being of the people. In one of his earliest
pronouncements on the subject he took sharp issue with
Dr. Benjamin M. Anderson, economist for the Chase National Bank, who had advocated letting the national economy right itself through the agency of "free markets."
Lippmann accused the economist of dealing with an imag-
inary world and ignoring the realities of "contracts, gentlemen's agreements, ... monopolies, trade union rules, legislation and other devices for interfering with the law of
supply and demand." [6]

Lippmann went to great lengths to explain that he was
not in favor of a "planned economy." During the first two
and a half years of the New Deal he did not seem to feel
that such a scheme was being advanced by the Administration. "I do not regard the Roosevelt program as directed
to the establishment of a planned economy," he said. [7] In

this period Lippmann found Mr. Roosevelt's "planning" quite acceptable, for it appeared to involve only the "conscious management of many things, an unwillingness to drift, and prudent, orderly thinking.[8] The commentator came out for social-security legislation, arguing that "this is the proper time to make a national commitment to establish protection against the hazards of unemployment, of sickness, old age, of technological displacement, of sweating and exploitation."[9]

In the Edwin Lawrence Godkin lectures delivered at Harvard in May, 1934, and published as *The Method of Freedom*,[10] Lippmann further clarified his views on the rôle of government in modern society. "The modern state," he declared, "cannot endure unless it insures to its people their standard of life. Only by making its people economically secure can a modern government have independence, wield influence in the world, preserve law, order, and liberty. That is now the central task of government, the very heart of statesmanship...."[11]

Laissez faire, he argued, was dead. The demands laid on modern governments made some kind of "collectivism" inevitable. But there was a choice between a "directed" economy and a "compensated" economy. To Lippmann the former meant absolutism, the latter a maximum of liberty. He frequently referred to "compensated" economy as "free collectivism." It was "collectivist" in that it was predicated on the clear responsibility of the state for the national welfare as a whole.[12] It was "free" in that private enterprise, within extensive limits, could still flourish.

The governments of the world, he said, had long exercised a supervisory function. They insured honest weights and measures, suppressed counterfeiting, regulated public utilities; they established minimum-wage laws, controlled monopolies, and discouraged harmful enterprises. But in our complex industrial order mere regulatory legislation had proved insufficient to prevent economic catastrophe. Something more was needed. A corrective force, powerful enough to offset the totality of individual decisions, had to be held in reserve for use when necessary. This power must be wielded by the state, which would become, in effect, "a gigantic public corporation." [13] It would spend when private industry was saving, and hoard when business was booming.

Having at its disposal the nation's resources, this "compensated" economy would utilize any of its instrumentalities to effect its purposes. A variable price for gold and silver, a managed currency, a huge reservoir of public works to be drawn upon when business was slack, a flexible tax rate which could be raised during boom periods and lowered when business fell off—all of these were useful means for keeping the nation's economy in balance.

To maintain a reasonably satisfactory equilibrium with respect to foreign nations, Lippmann provided for state control of international payments. "... tariffs and foreign credits can and should be treated as instruments for keeping the budget of international payments in approximate balance," he wrote.[14]

"Free collectivism," then, was Lippmann's middle course. It avoided the twin evils of governmental tyranny on one hand, and unrestrained laissez faire on the other. This "new social principle" which provided for both "individual initiative and collective initiative" was called by Lippmann "the method of freedom." The essence of the plan lay in his proposal that the "authority of the government is used to assist man in maintaining the security of an ordered life."

Under a "free collectivism," Lippmann said, private enterprise would thrive. This was of primary importance, because "private property was the original source of freedom." It was still, he added, freedom's main bulwark. A broad distribution of private property was necessary for the survival of liberty. The existence of a large proletariat without a vested interest in the economy constituted social danger. They were a constant temptation to the rich, who many times in the past had used them to subvert the government. In the fascist countries, he said, the plutocracy, by purchasing the support of the proletariat, had acquired control of the state.[15]

Strenuous efforts had therefore to be made to raise the proletariat to the "middle condition." For only when the middle group was numerous and thriving were our institutions safe. The attack, Lippmann specified, had to be made on proletarian poverty, not on plutocracy. No good could come from striking at the possessors of great wealth, for "a merely antiplutocratic policy is essentially vindictive and punitive; it does not make the mass of people any more secure to make the rich insecure...." [16]

The remedy lay elsewhere. Government, Lippmann emphasized, had a responsibility that went beyond the mere provision of education, housing, and insurance against unemployment, old age, and disability. These functions were "indispensable ... [but] inadequate...." The times called for something more: the opening of new frontiers of economic opportunity. Expressed in real terms this meant recognition by government of the right to remunerative employment. Lippmann proposed that a great pool of public works should always be available. When business slackened public projects should be initiated. These enterprises would have as their main objective the enrichment of the national patrimony. Lippmann cited the Civilian Conservation Corps and the Civil Works Administration as suggestive of the possibilities in this area. He recommended wages representing an "adequate minimum" locally. "By making them adequate for a bare but self-respecting existence, the oppression and sweating of labor is discouraged." [17]

This right to work, Lippmann felt, was of transcendent importance, and should, in fact, be added to "the rights of man." [18] The financing of work projects was a mere technical matter. They might be paid for out of savings and taxes or by borrowing and inflation, depending upon "whether the economic order ... required contraction or expansion to keep it in balance." [19]

All these elements taken together constituted Lipp-

mann's "free collectivism." That he regarded the New
Deal as embodying these principles is suggested in his
words, "... free collectivism, as indicated in the policies of
the English-speaking countries during the present crisis, is
the method of liberty in the Twentieth Century as laissez
faire was its method in the Nineteenth." [20]

Later Lippmann confirmed the principles elaborated in
Method of Freedom. In newspaper articles he emphasized
the rôle of government as a "balance wheel to private action," and repeated his view that economic opportunity
lay in artificially created public work. The New Deal, he
said, represented "the affirmative method which liberalism
has evolved as the alternative to the old deal, to communism and to fascism." [21] In the *New Imperative*,[22] published
in 1935, Lippmann found that Mr. Hoover's efforts to
relieve the effects of the depression had been in principle
the same as Mr. Roosevelt's. The responsibility of government to maintain a decent standard of living for all the
people was the "new imperative which takes its place
alongside the older imperatives to defend the nation
against attack and to preserve domestic peace." [23]

Toward the middle of 1935 Lippmann's writings about
the New Deal took on a new tone. While at the beginning
of the year he had described the Roosevelt program as
"the policy of a regenerated liberalism," the columnist by
summer was openly suspicious that the President was trying to substitute "some kind of planned collectivism for a
free economy." [24] Thereafter the commentator's hostility to
the New Deal showed a consistent development.

Lippmann's changed economic outlook had its fullest expression in *The Good Society*, which appeared in 1937 [25]
and was republished six years later. The two editions are
identical except for a new introduction in which Lippmann reaffirmed the book's thesis and in which, curiously,
he declared his belief that the book contained "more
truth than error." In many of his columns, and in various
other writings [26] Lippmann made clear his continuing belief in *Good Society's* basic argument: that "collectivism"

had become the supreme economic evil of our time; that only a return to what he called "liberalism" could free society.

The industrial revolution, he said, had made necessary the exchange of goods and services in the free market. There alone decisions could be reached as to production and distribution. These processes had become too complex to be brought under any over-all plan or direction. Buyer and seller coming to terms in the market place represented the basic reality in our modern economy. True "liberalism," accepting this fact, sought to improve the operation of the market but never to impair or restrict it.[27] But "collectivism," defined by Lippmann as governmental administration of large sectors of human affairs, either impeded or destroyed the working of the free market. For as the government asserted its control over various aspects of the national economy, the market was rendered increasingly inoperative. The worst aspect of such "collectivism" was its inevitable tendency to proliferate. It led, ultimately, to the total collectivism of fascism or communism.[28]

In about 1870, Lippmann argued, the liberals of that day reached a parting-of-the-ways on the means to combat the evils afflicting society. One group, called by Lippmann the "latter-day liberals," refused to recognize the existence of social and economic ills. They insisted on perpetuating the market economy as they had always known it, identifying liberalism with laissez faire. This group, claimed Lippmann, had come very close to grasping the key to modern industrial organization. If they had correctly interpreted Adam Smith and provided the remedial measures he favored, they could have preserved for the world the benefits of a free-market economy. In their blindness they had permitted the initiative to pass to another group of liberals, the "collectivists," who determined to use the state as an instrument for readjusting social and economic relationships.

These "collectivists," said Lippmann, had the "zest for progress, the sympathy for the poor, the burning sense of wrong, the impulse for great deeds, which have been lacking in latter-day liberalism." [29] Their influence on the western world was enormous. Known variously as "social democrats, Fabian socialists, evolutionary or revisionist socialists or merely progressives," they all employed the national government to effect far-reaching reforms.

Lippmann grouped various aspects of collectivism together and damned them all. Tariffs, bounties, fixed wages, fixed prices, and guaranteed incomes were typical "collectivist" interferences with the free operation of a market economy. Each was a restrictive measure enacted to appease a pressure group—businessmen, farmers, or labor. The certain consequences of such legislation were reduced output and the impoverishment of society. "...Old Guard Republicanism in the United States with its patronage of corporate collectivism, serves other interests than the collectivism of the New Deal. There are also important differences between lions and tigers...." Communists, fascists, and the adherents of the Second, Third, and Fourth internationals were included among the proscribed collectivists.[30] Lippmann conceded that "like the Capulets and the Montagues, they fight sincerely and furiously." But so far as he was concerned they were sub-species of the same genus. They all denied the premise that prosperity could be achieved through the unfettered operation of a market economy. In Lippmann's view the real conflict was not among the "collectivist" sects at all, but rather between true liberalism on one hand and all the collectivisms on the other.

The intellectuals who had introduced collectivist measures to cure genuine ills were actually responsible for launching their governments on the path of coercion, regimentation, and tyranny.[31] To engraft collectivist principles on the market economy was not to improve it but rather to commit it to certain, if slow death.[32]

Adam Smith, thought Lippmann, had discovered the basic truth of how a market economy must operate. He had seen that "the wealth of nations proceeds from the

division of labor in widening, and, therefore, freer markets." [33] Karl Marx, on the other hand, had concentrated
on the title deeds to property. He had mistakenly believed
that by transferring ownership of property from individuals to the nation, society would be reformed.[34] Marx,
said Lippmann, had missed the single important economic
fact of modern times, the law of the industrial revolution.
He had assumed, erroneously, that the evils associated with
modern industry could be cured by vesting ownership of
all property in the state; that the building of an elaborate
mechanism for regulating production and distribution
would somehow eliminate the admitted injustices of a
market economy. But, said Lippmann, Marx had failed
to sense that to control production was to inhibit it and
thereby to insure a declining standard of living. Coercion
had then to be employed in order to suppress discontent.
Marx was guilty of enlisting the "progressive sympathies
of the western world in a reactionary cause." [35] The restor-
ation by Lenin in 1921, and by Stalin in 1931, of an
"economy directed by the market" was cited by Lippmann
as proof that the exchange system alone was capable of
producing wealth in modern times.[36]

True liberalism, argued Lippmann, meant emancipa-
tion from restraints. It meant free science, the acceleration
of invention, the liberation of the spirit. He noted that
the century following the introduction of the division of
labor was marked by great social advances. Chattel slav-
ery, the subjection of women, the exploitation of backward
peoples, and the disfranchisement of the masses were
largely done away with in that period. These benefits were
the result of the "profitable exchange of specialized labor,"
of the harmonious functioning of "widely separated but
collaborating men and communities." [37]

Economic planning was the very essence of collectivism.
Lippmann admitted that it was necessary in time of war.
Military expediency then determined quantity and character of output and distribution. It was likewise possible,
even practical, to plan in a poor economy, where short-

ages prevailed. Because demand, under such conditions, outran supply, virtually the entire output of industry would be consumed. But peacetime planning in an economy of abundance he held to be a contradiction in terms. Where free choice existed it was impossible to foretell human wants. There would be shortages and glut at the same time. Moreover any plan adopted in a democratic country would be subject to revision by the electorate; an ever-changing plan would be no plan at all.[38] Arbitrariness and despotism would then have to be employed in order to force compliance. Planning, according to Lippmann, posed two highly unattractive choices: one, a chaotic society in which the "plan" was constantly being revised by a fickle people; the second, a tyranny in which despotic leaders would pressure their victims into conforming.

Aside from the fact that there were no men capable of planning for whole societies in peacetime, the "Good Society," he said, had no architectural design; it had neither blueprints nor molds. "To the liberal mind the notion that men can authoritatively plan and impose a good life upon a great society is ignorant, impertinent, and pretentious." [39]

Obviously this indictment was directed at the New Deal. For in the 1936 campaign Lippmann bluntly charged Mr. Roosevelt with having tried to install a planned economy, and of designing to consummate such a program if re-elected.[40]

Lippmann differentiated between "big" business and "collectivist" business. Enterprises that grew because they had expanded their activities under competitive conditions were working successfully according to the market economy. But businesses such as holding companies, that had combined to dominate operations and restrict competition were clearly "collectivist." The size of a corporation, therefore, was in itself indicative of little. Large industries that maintained their position in competition with other companies were operating within the exchange economy. But all "artificial" combinations designed to eliminate competition violated the principles of the free market.

There were two methods of social control, according to Lippmann. One was by means of government bureaucracy; the other by the application of the common law. The first was authoritarian and collectivist. In it, officials with near-sovereign power imposed their will upon the people. The "bureaucrats" tended to acquire a proprietary interest in their agencies and to lose all effective ties with the legislatures that had created them. The second possibility, favored by Lippmann, was control by a common law that defined the citizen's rights and invited him to enforce the law by proving his case in court.[41] He would give each individual a vested interest in the law, placing the initiative for enforcement in the hands of those who believed themselves injured.

The administration of justice, said Lippmann, was within the ability of man; the ordering and planning of large portions of human affairs were beyond it. Through recourse to the law, rather than to the "officialdom" of authoritarian states, individuals would adjust their relations with each other.[42] While he encouraged settlement of disputes out of court, he nevertheless admitted that his program would make necessary "many more tribunals." [43]

Rejecting the notion that corporations were immune from the law, Lippmann held that charters were merely licenses subject to whatever conditions the sovereign state saw fit to include. By specifying the provisions under which a charter was granted, the state could exercise a high degree of regulation.[44] If the state could establish in court that a corporation had violated the terms of its charter, the franchise could be withdrawn. That which the law granted it could, under appropriate conditions, retrieve, for "there is no such thing as an absolute, illimitable, and indefeasible system of property rights." [45]

Generally, Lippmann said, monopolies existed by virtue of a legal privilege of some kind. His remedy for their abuses: "monopoly can be destroyed and prevented by changing the law." [46] He felt, it would seem, that to out-law undesirable practices was to eliminate them. He was ignoring the whole tortuous history of governmental efforts to make monopolies conform to existing laws.

More difficult to understand was Lippmann's proposal that regulatory commissions should be supplanted by "law." [47] This meant that an individual, when he believed himself wronged, and able to prove his case in court, would bring suit. By this means, Lippmann suggested, corporations could be held to the law. Lippmann expected individuals to fight corporations in the courts and believed, apparently, that such adversaries would have equal chances of prevailing before the law. [48] This cheerful—and mechan-ical—conception of justice bears little resemblance to the realities of legal procedure.

Lippmann's distrust of bureaus and their administrators did not blind him to the need for government administration of certain social services. He emphatically repudiated laissez faire, calling it a disease that had overtaken liberalism. He argued that our market economy could not be expected to operate with justice to everyone. There were too many evil possibilities to trust to laissez faire. Adam Smith, he maintained, had never advocated a complete hands-off policy, and neither did he. Those critics who called *Good Society* a defense of laissez faire economics had never read beyond the first hundred pages of the book, he noted with contempt. [49]

Calling his program of needed reforms the "Agenda of Liberalism," [50] Lippmann said it would mitigate the hardships of a free economy. It would improve the economic position of those groups who normally suffered disadvantages: the worker who had only his labor to sell, the farmer who was innocent of the workings of the market, the consumer who did not know the real merits of the commodities he was urged to buy. It was part of the "Agenda" to extend and improve education, to furnish the recreational facilities needed by a modern people, to conserve the country's natural resources. Great public works designed

to improve waterways, insure the fertility of the soil, prevent flood and erosion, and preserve our forests and
parks were appropriate government enterprises. Those
workers, moreover, who lost their jobs because of technological advances or the movement of industry should be
indemnified. Above all, true liberalism must be recognized
as the opponent of all practices, whether of industry or
labor, that restricted the free working of our market economy. Holding companies and monopolies would therefore
be outlawed. Liberalism, he emphasized, was neither the
defender of the status quo nor the friend of privilege.

To pay for the social reforms he advocated, Lippmann
urged a taxation program that would strike most heavily
at "unearned" income. He admitted the difficulties of en-
forcing such a policy but maintained that it alone was designed for the market economy. Earnings reinvested in
competitive industry would be subject to relatively low
rates, but unearned income not so invested would be
heavily taxed. The equalization of incomes by such a plan
was a "necessary objective" of a liberal policy. At the same
time Lippmann emphasized his opposition to "a mere
leveling of incomes" as destructive of a free economy. The
purpose of the equalization was to strike "not at the profits
of successful competition but at the tolls of monopoly." [51]

Granting that there was a legitimate realm of government activity embracing social services and public works,
Lippmann was nevertheless concerned to see that the duly
constituted agencies did not aggrandize power. Regularly
chartered bureaus had to be held strictly accountable to
the law. Administrators had to exercise those functions
that were enumerated in their charters but not go beyond
them. The state, as judge and conciliator, had under no
conditions to merge its identity with the bureaus, for that
would be not the delegation of authority but rather the
abdication of responsibility.[52] Bureau heads, according to
the "liberal" concept, had to be subordinate to the state,
and on a basis of equality with the citizens. The insignia
and power of office could confer on them no special rights.

Their actions had at all times to be subject to review and their position must never be touched with sovereignty.[53]

Lippmann emphasized repeatedly that public servants, including legislators and executives of all degrees, should cultivate a "judicial" temperament. Men, he thought, had the capacity to decide between alternatives; but they were not capable of national planning in peacetime. "...the primary task of liberal statesmanship is to judge the claims of particular interests asking a revision of the laws, and to endeavor amidst these conflicting claims to make equitable decisions." [54]

The program of reform enumerated in Lippmann's "Agenda of Liberalism" sounds very much like the objectives of the New Deal. But Lippmann's proposals were to be carried out under conditions of a free market, in a society where "the law" was supreme, where there was no baneful bureaucracy, and where the necessary officials possessed the "judicial" temperament.

Surely Lippmann was asking here for the impossible— a "free market" and a New Dealish "Agenda of Liberalism." His alarm over the "collectivist" New Deal is incompatible with the responsibilities he assigned to government in countless newspaper articles, in *Method of Freedom,* in *The New Imperative,* and—it must be said—in *Good Society* itself. Perhaps the phrase "collectivism" began, after 1935, to convey to him some special, nightmarish quality. At least through 1934, however, he did not object to it. The record is clear that in *Method of Freedom* he had advocated a "free collectivism"; in *Good Society,* on the other hand, he inveighed against all "collectivisms."

Lippmann's lumping of New Deal reformism with Communism and Fascism can hardly have enlightened his readers. And his exaltation of a puristic society under "law," governed by men with the "judicial" temperament can only have stirred discontent with the human efforts of Mr. Roosevelt to preserve republican institutions while mastering a shattering economic crisis.

LIPPMANN AND
PRESIDENT FRANKLIN D. ROOSEVELT

WHAT WALTER LIPPMANN TOLD HIS READERS ABOUT Franklin D. Roosevelt and the New Deal has been charted by the use of "content categories." [1] A "content category" is a subject with relatively well-defined limits, such as an act of Congress: the National Industrial Recovery Act, the Social Security Act, and the Wagner Act are examples. The use of the content category makes it possible to show clearly Mr. Lippmann's attitude on specific issues. It introduces a needed element of definiteness in a field notoriously susceptible to subjective judgments.

For the years 1932 to 1938 every reference Lippmann made in his "Today and Tomorrow" column to the President or to New Deal measures was studied. The examination was concentrated on this period because it was a time of great economic and social stress. During these years the bulk of the controversial New Deal legislation was proposed and enacted; after 1938 Mr. Roosevelt—and Mr. Lippmann—devoted themselves increasingly to foreign affairs.

Lippmann's statements about the President and his program were divided into three groups: "favorable," "unfavorable," and "neutral." When Lippmann expressed approval of a measure, a tally was entered in the "favorable" column; when he opposed a measure he was recorded as "unfavorable"; when he presented a "balanced" view or was non-committal he was put down as "neutral." Only those references were tabulated in which Lippmann expressed a definite "value judgment" or personal opinion. Mere incidental mentions of the President or his measures were not included in the tabulations.

The table below shows the "favorable," "unfavorable," and "neutral" references made by the columnist to Mr. Roosevelt in the years 1932-1938.

LIPPMANN'S REFERENCES TO FRANKLIN D. ROOSEVELT (1932-1938)

	Favorable	Unfavorable	Neutral
Number:	13	61	46
Per Cent:	11	51	38

Lippmann looked with disfavor on the 1932 candidacy of Franklin D. Roosevelt. This attitude softened after the election, and for a little over two years the columnist was rather friendly. Toward the end of 1935, however, he began to show mounting hostility to the President and his practices.

Writing as early as January 8, 1932, Lippmann found Governor Roosevelt lacking in the qualities required of a Presidential candidate. "...Franklin D. Roosevelt is no crusader. He is no tribune of the people. He is no enemy of entrenched privilege. He is a pleasant man who, without any important qualifications for the office, would very much like to be President." [2] Lippmann conceded, however, that the Presidential aspirant's views on public utilities and the tariff, as expressed in a St. Paul speech, were sound.

Primary-election disappointments for Mr. Roosevelt in Massachusetts and Pennsylvania provided occasion for further headshaking by the columnist:

...the people of the East know about Mr. Roosevelt, and gradually have taken his measure. They just do not believe in him. They have detected something hollow in him, something synthetic, something pretended and calculated. While they are far from having definite ideas as to what the policies of the country ought to be, they would like the next President to ring true. Mr. Roosevelt does not ring true. This has been the judgment of the great majority of Democratic insiders. It has now been confirmed by the urban masses of the East.[3]

Several times during this period Lippmann charged that Governor Roosevelt had been compromised by his relations with Tammany Hall. The columnist found that the "trouble with Franklin D. Roosevelt is that his mind is not very clear, his purposes are not simple, and his methods are not direct."[4] Despite these harsh words, the columnist had voted for gubernatorial-candidate Roosevelt in 1928 and again in 1930.[5]

Lippmann was not without a candidate of his own. With considerable eloquence he pleaded the cause of Newton D. Baker, whom he advanced as the perfect nominee. It is not surprising, therefore, that the naming of Roosevelt disappointed the columnist, who lamented that among Herbert Hoover, Franklin Roosevelt, and Norman Thomas there was no "ideal" candidate. As the campaign progressed, however, Lippmann's hostility to Roosevelt lessened, and by September 27, 1932 the columnist was criticizing a *Herald Tribune* editorial that impugned the Governor's courage. Hoover, the columnist declared, had shown neither courage nor candor in his association with the Harding cabinet. Roosevelt's trafficking with Tammany, said Lippmann, was not materially worse. The failing of the Democratic candidate "is the weakness which he shares with Mr. Hoover in common with the run of American public men: he is too ambitious and he is too anxious to win."[6]

A month before the election Lippmann announced that he would "cheerfully" vote for Roosevelt. The Republicans, he explained, had been isolationist; they had increased exports while barring the manufactured goods of other countries. They had encouraged foreigners to buy and borrow while making repayment almost impossible.

By drawing "half the monetary gold of the world into the United States," they had "laid the foundation of the great inflation of the Twenties." Roosevelt, on the other hand, was showing a competence hitherto unrevealed. Finally, Lippmann pointed out, there would be a Democratic Congress, and with Roosevelt in the Presidency unity and discipline might be achieved.[7]

A few days before the nation went to the polls Lippmann criticized Hoover for using scare tactics. Calling the roll of projected Democratic reforms, Lippmann declared them to be entirely consistent with long-time American development, and designed "to make the public interest paramount over private acquisitiveness in the direction of the vital services of American life." [8]

After the election Lippmann wrote a series of articles in which he urged the President-elect to act with speed and decisiveness in meeting the national crisis.[9] He recommended that Roosevelt "employ the caucus resolutely and ... back its decisions by withholding the patronage until its decisions are obeyed." For the recalcitrant Congressmen there should be "a birch rod in the closet." [10] Lippmann demanded that for a year the new President be given the broadest possible powers, with the rules of both houses temporarily suspended, the right of amendment and debate sharply limited, and the majority in both houses under absolute party discipline.

The President-elect, said the columnist, had received a mandate from the people. Their clearly expressed wishes must be translated into a vigorous, uncompromising legislative program. To those who feared that the President might acquire dictatorial powers, Lippmann pointed out that the Chief Executive would still be bound by Constitutional restrictions and that his party would have to face the electorate within two years.[11]

The President's Cabinet choices excited little admiration in Lippmann. He regarded them as adequate, but far from brilliant.[12] Nevertheless, hardly two weeks after the inaugural Lippmann felt there had been a national recapture of morale, comparable to the "second battle of the Marne in the summer of 1918." [13] To the President's firm leadership went the credit.

Thereafter Lippmann repeatedly approved Roosevelt's efforts to achieve both recovery and reform. Answering an accusation by Ogden Mills that the President was setting up a "planned economy," Lippmann pointed out that Mr. Hoover, too, had had to do a certain amount of planning for public works, for farm-price stabilization, and for "re-flating" price levels. Essentially, thought Lippmann, Mr. Roosevelt's program represented an extension of such policies rather than a "planned economy." [14]

Appraising the Administration after a year in office, Lippmann thought it deserved commendation. Especially noteworthy, the columnist declared, were the President's organization of political leadership, his revaluation of the dollar, and the "pumping out of funds to consumers of goods." [15]

By April 26, 1934, however, Lippmann found the Administration working at cross purposes. Speaking of the plans to prevent abuses in the money market, Lippmann thought the proposed reforms were so severe as to inhibit financial enterprise. By the summer of 1934 Lippmann seemed to feel there had been changes enough for a while and he expressed the view that "private initiative" required a "sense of certainty," and a stabilization of government power.[16]

The beginning of the following year, though, found the columnist warmly approving the President's proposal to launch a great public-works program and end the Federal dole. Such a policy signified the difference between our system, where government intervention was "a balance wheel to private action," and socialism. "This is the only course by which a nation like ours can today hope to achieve that security which the President promises and still retain all those fundamental liberties to which he is devoted." [17]

The honeymoon period was nevertheless drawing to a

close. Writing during the summer of 1935 on the Holding-Company Bill, Lippmann condemned the Administration for insisting on the Senate version of the measure. Lippmann argued that the difference between House and Senate bills was "insubstantial." Yet, under the Senate bill, the burden of proof was placed upon the holding company. It had to prove to the Securities and Exchange Commission and to the courts that it should not be dissolved. But under the House bill the Commission was required to prove that the holding company should be dissolved.[18] That Lippmann, a serious student of economic problems, could find this issue unimportant is in itself a notable fact. In an earlier article he had written in favor of the holding-company measure as "a revival of old-fashioned, hundred per cent American trust busting applied to the complicated and gigantic trusts of the new era that preceded the New Deal."[19] Despite these unequivocal words he seemed willing to accept a defective reform measure. Later he again attacked the Administration for its insistence on a strong bill.[20]

Lippmann followed shortly after with sharp criticism of the President's newly introduced "soak-the-rich" tax plan, arguing that a hot and tired Congress, eager to adjourn, should not be held in Washington to wrestle with added legislation. In addition Lippmann cautioned that "an overpowering desire for the improvement of society leads to policies which put too great a strain on institutions, which transcend the administrative capacity of officials, which surpass the understanding of the people."[21] Showing an increasing restiveness with the direction being taken by the President, the columnist asked finally whether Mr. Roosevelt had in mind to substitute "some kind of planned collectivism for a free economy." To this query Lippmann added an emphatic declaration that the emergency was over.[22]

By year's end, Lippmann's normally restrained language was becoming more vigorous, betraying, especially where Mr. Roosevelt was concerned, considerable depth of feeling. The columnist maintained, for example, that in considering farm relief the President had sought in every way to help the farmer, offering compensation in return for cooperation. But when dealing with industry and finance the President had "resorted to coercive laws, to threats, to punishment, to 'death sentences.' "

Lippmann charged that while Mr. Roosevelt had sought only to assist the farmer, he had tried to "overawe" the businessman. "In the case of agriculture, the spirit has been that of a partner; in the case of industry the spirit has been that of a stern mentor, often that of a prosecutor, and in some instances that of a persecutor." [23] Thereafter Lippmann exhibited growing alarm at what he took to be the centralizing tendencies of the Administration, the persistent arrogation to itself of power.

In an article detailing the differences between Senator William E. Borah and the President, the columnist pictured the Senator as an "individualist who opposes all concentration of power, political or economic, who is against political bureaucracy and centralized government." Mr. Borah was credited with believing in the supremacy of the law, and with insisting that the government itself was accountable to the law. Mr. Roosevelt, however, was said to have "no such instinctive appreciation of American liberalism in this, its oldest and most authentic sense." He was "not much concerned about the old safeguards of liberty." His primary interest, on the other hand, was in obtaining enough power to provide economic security for all the people. Lippmann compared the President to a paternalistic "Tory philanthropist" who was more disposed to help the people than to let them help themselves.[24] This analogy, it should be noted, followed earlier discussions in which the columnist had applauded the President's decision to provide work relief—that is, self-help—rather than a dole.[25] A more serious misreading of the President's purpose is hard to imagine. Nor is it easy to picture a "Tory philanthropist" launching a WPA. A

handout would seem to be a more likely form of benefac-
tion.

As the 1936 national nominating conventions drew
closer, Lippmann emphasized repeatedly that Mr. Roosevelt was leading the nation into a collectivist order alien to
American traditions and repugnant to the American
people. He appeared to be convinced that the President's
basic design was to install a "planned economy." The columnist held, moreover, that Roosevelt was willing to match
the monopoly position of industry by bestowing monopoly
privileges on both agriculture and labor.[26] The President
had worked himself into an impossible position by his "collectivism" and his relief expenditures. Citing the National
Industrial Recovery Act, the Agricultural Adjustment Act,
and the Guffey Coal Act as evidence of "collectivism,"
Lippmann declared that the country would not tolerate
such adventures. He argued that we were in danger of
being "permanently committed, even with full recovery,
to annual Federal payments of two billions or so to the
needy...." Lippmann's solution, which is difficult to rec-
oncile with his earlier statements on the subject of local
versus Federal relief, was "a drastic reduction of the Federal funds, which will force the responsibility back upon
the localities, upon families and upon individuals."[27]

Deeply disturbing to Lippmann was the "supineness" of
the Democratic National Convention in permitting the
President to "redirect" the party's course.[28] The columnist's assertions were free of any reminder that the President's recommendations would have to run the gauntlet
of Congressional debate and approval, and that the electorate would ultimately decide whether Mr. Roosevelt's
doctrines were attuned to the country's needs.

The President's acceptance speech at Franklin Field,
Philadelphia, was discussed by the columnist in an article
titled "Right About Face."[29] Mr. Roosevelt, said Lippmann, alert to the renewed interest in "free" as against
"planned" economy, had made a strategic retreat when he
asked for old-fashioned "progressivism" instead of "collec-

tivism." This, said Lippmann, was an act of shrewdness; it showed that the President sensed the popular revulsion to centralization.

Nevertheless, on September 8, 1936 the columnist announced that Alf Landon was his choice for President. Lippmann charged that Roosevelt, though he had given brilliant leadership, had sinned grieviously: he had dropped from the party councils all who hadn't supported him before the 1932 Chicago convention; he had ignored the Republicans; he had "conducted his Administration as a personal, factional and partisan enterprise." Landon, if elected, would of course have to deal with a Democratic Congress. But this would be an advantage, for the President would then have to form a national, bipartisan government; persuasion and co-operation would necessarily follow. The old checks and balances would replace "mere majority rule under personal leadership." [30] It is relevant at this point to recall that in 1932 Lippmann had argued against the re-election of Hoover on the grounds that the Congress would be Democratic. The columnist had predicted paralysis in government if Hoover won.[31] Now, four years later, he insisted that bi-party government under Landon would be a blessing.

Summarizing his case for and against the President, Lippmann approved the early embargo on gold which had made possible the refunding of debts at lower interest; the strengthening of the commercial banking structure; the modernizing of the Federal Reserve System; the regulation of the capital market; the recently enacted international currency agreement. But he condemned NRA, AAA, and above all the "spending program" which in his view should have been effected through the states. Instead, he argued, the President had used it as an instrument of political aggrandizement.[32]

The Democratic candidate was not the sole object of Lippmann's criticism. At least twice he chided Landon for seeking to outbid Roosevelt in his appeals to the electorate.[33] The whole purpose of Landon's candidacy, Lippmann asserted, was to rally the people who opposed the paternalistic concept of government. For Landon and his lieutenants to offer government largesse as a means of attracting votes was a violation of first principles. Lippmann also opposed Republican Vice-presidential candidate Colonel Knox's attempts to alarm investors, and Republican Chairman Hamilton's use of the Red issue.[34]

But Lippmann continued to stress the importance of checking Roosevelt, at the very least by substantially increasing Republican membership in the House.

For nothing could be worse for Mr. Roosevelt, or for the Democratic party, or for the country, than another Democratic landslide. For Mr. Roosevelt it would be the kind of personal triumph which in human nature generally, and in his nature particularly, does not make for judgment and magnanimity. For the Democratic party, a landslide would give a great impetus to its transformation from a national to a sectional and class organization. And for the country, it would mean that instead of a responsible opposition in Washington which voiced the grievances of the minority, there would be an irresponsible opposition devoted to mere agitation.[35]

That a landslide might also indicate decisive popular approval of Mr. Roosevelt's record was not mentioned as a possibility.

Two days later Lippmann's "Today and Tomorrow" column carried an article in which he gave a most curious reason for repudiating the New Deal. A "visitor from abroad" had explained to the columnist that in modern warfare the tendency was to strike swift, paralyzing blows at the heart, that is, the capital, of a country, and by so doing create wide confusion and speedy capitulation. In the United States, Lippmann added, there was a fortunate dispersion of economic, industrial, and cultural resources. Since all centralizing tendencies were prejudicial to the national security in this air age, they should be carefully avoided. The obvious conclusion was to reject the New Deal.[36]

Writing after the election, Lippmann attributed Mr.

Roosevelt's success to "good times," and pronounced the ungenerous judgment that he had won not because "the people have any special belief in his policies, but because they approve of the result." [37] In a further elaboration a few days later, Lippmann explained that three factors had contributed to Mr. Roosevelt's victory: his handling of the gold question, his yielding to Secretary Hull's views on the tariff, and the opportune decision of the Supreme Court invalidating NRA.[38]

The Republican Party, Lippmann declared, had "entered this campaign with the fatal delusion in its high command that it could win. That was never possible." The Republicans had begun with a great idea, "the maintenance of a free, competitive capitalism under a decentralized government of limited powers." But in their eagerness to capture votes the Republicans had compromised their principles, not scorning to use the "bank scare, the insurance scare, the red scare, the social security scare...." Thereby, said the commentator, the Party had offended the "enlightened" and made clear its bankruptcy.[39] Lippmann's pre-election articles had scarcely suggested such serious doubts as to the purposes and strategy of the Republican Party or its leaders.

On February 5, 1937 President Roosevelt submitted to Congress his historic plan for reorganizing the Supreme Court. His most important recommendation was that he be empowered to appoint another judge for each Supreme Court judge over seventy who failed to retire, up to a maximum of fifteen judges.

In defense of his proposal the President declared:

I defy anyone to read the opinions concerning A.A.A., the railroad retirement act, the national recovery act, the Guffey coal act and the New York minimum wage law, and tell us exactly what, if anything, we can do for the industrial worker ... with any reasonable certainty that what we do will not be nullified as unconstitutional ... I defy anyone to read the opinions in the T.V.A. case or the Duke power case and tell us exactly what we can do ... to control flood and drought and

generate cheap power ... that will not be nullified as unconstitutional.[40]

Lippmann's reaction to Mr. Roosevelt's project was
strong and hostile. He flayed the President for what he
considered the ultimate step in the centralization of
power. The President's scheme was basically "stupid," he
thought, for with both a Congress and a Court "subserv-
ient" to his will, the people's confidence would be alienated. The Government itself would become suspect.[41] The
President's court scheme, though technically legal, violated
the spirit of the law.[42] The New Dealers, the columnist
added, were not interested in liberalizing the courts, any-
way. What they really sought was "to become the masters
of the courts in order that constitutional limitations and
judicial restraint may no longer check their own authority."[43] They were, in fact, "drunk with power."

Shortly before Mr. Roosevelt had introduced his court
plan Lippmann had emphatically agreed with the President that an "enlightened interpretation" of the Constitution, rather than its amendment, was needed. The commentator could conceive of no amendment wide enough
to validate necessary social legislation without destroying
all limits on Congressional powers.[44]

But once the President announced his court proposal,
Lippmann quickly became enthusiastic about a variety
of amendments that would, he thought, solve the problem. The Constitution should be amended so that the
commerce clause could be changed bit by bit, as necessary.[45] Senator Borah's plan to deny the Supreme Court's
right to review the substance of state laws was a good idea,
too. An amendment was also needed, said Lippmann, to
facilitate the transfer of powers from the states to the Federal government for given periods of time. He favored
an amendment providing for compulsory retirement of
judges at the age of seventy.[46] A week later he approved
the idea of making the amending process easier "where
it affects the powers reserved to the states." In the same

article he commended the Wheeler-Bone amendment by which two-thirds of Congress could re-pass a measure invalidated by the Supreme Court, provided a national election had taken place in the interval. He also favored the Norris proposal to prevent the Court from invalidating acts of Congress by less than a 7 to 2 vote.[47]

These were Lippmann's constructive alternatives to the President's plan. As a student of judicial problems, Lippmann recognized as a "flagrant" abuse the "nullifying of state laws under the due process clause of the Fourteenth Amendment."[48] But he would have none of Mr. Roosevelt's solution. He went so far as to predict that unless the President's program were halted, other actions, more "astounding" than the court scheme would follow. They would deal, the commentator guessed, "with the last remaining obstacle to the undisputed power of the Administration," namely, freedom of the press. "The logic of Mr. Roosevelt's philosophy today points to the hypothesis that, in order to attain his ends, he must somehow muzzle the press as he would like to pack the court."[49]

Lippmann charged that the Administration was shamelessly using patronage to coerce recalcitrant Congressmen into supporting the court plan. The Administration bill "is not a party measure but a personal measure, forced down the throats of the Democrats."[50] He defended the filibuster as a means of preventing the Administration from "conscripting" the votes of unwilling Senators.[51]

Affecting the President, said Lippmann, was "the intoxication of personal power." Mr. Roosevelt wished personally to make the laws, control public expenditures, rule the administrative and quasi-judicial commissions, dominate the courts and interpret the Constitution. This was personal government; it could lead only "from arbitrariness through confusion to tyranny."[52] The President thought of himself "not as a constitutional chief magistrate but as a specially selected leader enjoying some special and almost mystic inspiration from the subconscious wisdom of the crowd."[53] The columnist took occasion again to remind Mr. Roosevelt that "transient popular majorities, however impressive," could not give "to any American President a personal mandate to rule the country." [54]

Lippmann wanted the judiciary issue resolved in such a way that the Court would not be enlarged and Mr. Roosevelt not be shorn of his prestige. The President after all, conceded Lippmann, was not "a dictator like Mussolini or Hitler." He was, indeed, a "well-intentioned and charming gentleman" who needed, above everything else, "a little humility."

Here, then, stood Lippmann vis-a-vis the President: a grudging admiration for Mr. Roosevelt's daring and energy, coupled with a dread that he harbored dictatorial ambitions. While Lippmann sympathized with the President's humanitarian purposes, he feared that a collectivist order would attend their fulfillment.

Personal relations between the two men, while of long standing, at no time became intimate. Lippmann never hesitated to disagree with Mr. Roosevelt, though usually in intellectual rather than personal terms. The President, on the other hand, never very gracious about criticism, is known to have made many hostile remarks about the commentator.

Mr. Lippmann's friends deplored the President's failure to use the columnist's talents. But Mr. Roosevelt could hardly have been expected to embrace an outspoken critic. From time to time Lippmann adopted a lofty tone toward the President, thereby widening the breach between them. He declared, for example, that Mr. Roosevelt's "errors, . . . his false turnings, his alarming excursions into centralized collectivism arise not from a conspiracy . . . but from a lack of education in the experience of the past and a rather easy-going acceptance of fashionable ideas and . . . plausible schemes." [55]

Some of these "fashionable ideas" and "plausible schemes," as the next chapter indicates, appealed to Lippmann, too—until they were put into operation.

CHAPTER FIVE

LIPPMANN AND THE NEW DEAL

A S THE TABLE BELOW INDICATES, LIPPMANN'S REFERENCES to the New Deal as a whole in the years 1933 through 1938 were mostly unfavorable. For about the first two years of this period his sympathies rose and fell; sometimes he was for, sometimes against the Roosevelt legislative program. In the final years he was almost consistently hostile.

LIPPMANN'S REFERENCES TO THE NEW DEAL (1933-1938)

	Favorable	Unfavorable	Neutral
Number:	5	38	11
Per cent:	9	70	20

Early in 1934 he wrote a column in which he twitted his fellow columnist, Mark Sullivan, who had professed to see "socialism" spreading in this country. Lippmann pointed out that when Theodore Roosevelt had been called a socialist, Sullivan had helped to expose the emptiness of the charge. Significantly, however, Lippmann concluded his article by stating that there had been reforms enough for a while, that the country needed time to digest those already enacted.[1]

Shortly thereafter Lippmann again took occasion to refute the view that the New Deal was tending toward either communism or fascism. He found, rather, that the New Deal was most appropriately likened to "Theodore

Roosevelt's New Nationalism and Woodrow Wilson's New Freedom." Lippmann's defense of the New Deal, however, was not calculated to evoke pure gratitude from the President's supporters. For while Lippmann felt at this time that the New Deal was surmounting the crisis, he tempered his approval with the observation that the citizen now had "to pay more taxes than he likes to pay," and that "the new rules are puzzling and often somewhat foolish." [2]

Doubts about the New Deal continued to develop. The columnist maintained that the program had numerous contradictions, that New Deal measures were canceling each other out. He charged that while our delegation at the London Economic Conference was seeking to negotiate tariff reductions, policies of the National Industrial Recovery Administration precluded any such action; that whereas the Agricultural Adjustment Act was designed to give to farm prices parity with industrial prices, NRA caused industrial prices to rise; that the government's program to "prime the pump" was based on a scale of prices and wages so high as to discourage the revival of private construction.[3] Nevertheless, in an article called "The New Deal of Today" Lippmann stated categorically that " ... this is the policy of a regenerated liberalism, this is the affirmative method which liberalism has evolved as the alternative to the old deal, to communism and to fascism." [4]

The columnist clearly dissociated himself from the Roosevelt program in the words, "If the New Deal is the whole collection of measures hastily enacted in 1933 and 1934, I am not a New Dealer. But I do wish the President of the United States to succeed in what I take to be his effort to preserve the essentials of a free social order in the midst of a world-wide upheaval." [5]

A scant two months later the commentator was telling the New Dealers and their "twin brothers of the Old Guard" that "reflation—not planning, not regimentation, and not laissez faire—is the remedy for this depression." Lippmann described "reflation" as "deliberate government deficit expenditures financed by loans to augment the general purchasing power of the community."[6] To many observers deficit financing had seemed to be at the very heart of the New Deal—and Lippmann's criticism petulant and gratuitous. Subsequently Lippmann carried further his opposition to the President's policies, maintaining that through NRA and AAA they were extending monopoly to areas where it had never existed before. He regarded the Supreme Court's invalidation of NRA and AAA as a victory for the democratic process in that it had stopped the New Dealers' plans to change our economic system.[7]

Though his references to Roosevelt's program grew steadily more antagonistic, Lippmann insisted that the indictment of the New Deal drawn at the 1936 Republican National Convention at Cleveland was unbalanced. He criticized the failure "to weigh the evidence, to recognize the difficulties, to acknowledge the achievements."[8] He thereupon resumed his attack on the New Deal, professing to see in it a plan to establish a single standard of morals for the whole country, to be enforced from Washington. The New Deal, with its Federal regulation of wages, prices, and working conditions, imposed an impossible burden on the national government. The inevitable result would be "corruption, confusion, bureaucracy, racketeering, and bootlegging on a far greater scale than resulted from Federal Prohibition."[9]

In a radio speech describing the 1936 national conventions, Lippmann pronounced the New Deal dead, a victim of Supreme Court decisions. National recovery had been achieved in spite of, and not because of the New Deal. He also declared that the President had now turned his back on the "collectivism" of the 1933 New Deal, and had begun to advocate old-fashioned "progressivism," which the American people had always supported.[10]

There is good reason to believe that Lippmann doubted his own words as to the demise of the New Deal. For in subsequent articles he continued his attack, urging the electorate to repudiate New Deal "planning" and "centralization of power."[11] The New Dealers, he declared, had abandoned any pretense at even-handed enforcement of law. "They think of themselves as the leaders of a radical farmer-labor party." [12] Those who believed in their objectives, he concluded, were forced to oppose their methods. [13]

As the following sections show, Lippmann's unfavorable opinion of the New Deal as a whole reflected his feelings about most of the individual New Deal measures.

LIPPMANN AND THE FIRST AGRICULTURAL ADJUSTMENT ACT

Lippmann wrote with restrained approval of the First Agricultural Adjustment Act, designed to raise farm income by limiting production. In his earliest discussion of it he minimized its importance, stating that its probable effects were too insignificant to justify Congressional haggling over its terms. He felt that the measure would appear to be a success only if the major economic policies of the Administration achieved their goals. Failing this, AAA would not bring higher farm prices.

LIPPMANN'S REFERENCES TO THE FIRST AAA (1933-1938)

	Favorable	Unfavorable	Neutral
Number:	2	19	9
Per cent:	7	63	30

The columnist commended the "spirit of candid experimentation" in which the President offered the measure, and urged its adoption so that more important business might be reached. He assured his readers that there were no elements of "revolution" in the AAA program, and that it would be liquidated as soon as substantial recovery had been achieved. [14] A few months later he found AAA promoting scarcity and high prices and thereby neutralizing the government's monetary policies. [15] Nevertheless he deplored the action of the Circuit Court of Appeals when it declared processing taxes unconstitutional. For the Court's view to stand would constitute a disaster for American agriculture. He looked to the Supreme Court to reassert the right of Congress to legislate a national agricultural program.

Answering an attack on AAA by Mark Sullivan, Lippmann showed why agriculture needed protection: the farmer sold his produce at prices fixed in a world market but bought the things he needed in a highly protected market. Since manufacturers could profitably limit output, why not the farmer? Lippmann reminded his fellow commentator that Mr. Hoover, too, had had a farm program "based on essentially the same principle of government intervention against free markets." [16]

After the Supreme Court invalidated AAA in 1936 Lippmann reaffirmed the power of the Federal government to protect its agricultural resources. He justified the Court's action, however, on the grounds that AAA had become too intimately involved "in local and personal affairs" and had thereby exceeded Federal jurisdiction.[17] But the soil conservation program that succeeded AAA received Lippmann's hearty approval. He liked the idea that farmers would no longer be paid not to produce, and that soil-saving crops would be grown. He underscored the danger to the nation of allowing our agricultural potential to run down.[18]

But AAA seemed to become worse in retrospect than it had been in reality. The columnist began to regard it as a violation of the anti-monopoly clause of the 1932 platform, and as promoting a "planned economy." Finally he decided it was a "collectivist" measure.[19] The indictment was thereby made complete.

LIPPMANN AND THE NATIONAL INDUSTRIAL RECOVERY ACT

Save for a few friendly references directly following the enactment of the National Industrial Recovery Act, Lippmann was uniformly hostile to this measure. A far-reaching plan to stabilize industry, end price-cutting, and strengthen labor, NRA grew increasingly objectionable to the columnist. Its "centralization" of power and its "planning" represented, he said, an abandonment of traditional American principles.

LIPPMANN'S REFERENCES TO NRA (1933-1938)

	Favorable	*Unfavorable*	*Neutral*
Number:	2	32	4
Per cent:	5	84	11

His earliest criticisms had to do with the methods being used to induce businessmen to accept the NRA codes. Lippmann protested that Administration "propaganda" was creating a hysteria that might result in serious reprisals against the small businessmen who couldn't afford to comply with the codes.[20]

Lippmann's strongest statements in support of NRA appeared in his column of November 7, 1933. He declared his preference for government regulation as embodied in NRA to the previous system of government prosecution under anti-trust laws. "... in spite of all the tactical errors and superficial misconceptions of the first few months, NRA is almost certain to mark a permanent and basic change in industrial control." [21]

Thereafter the columnist's views on NRA became less sympathetic. He felt that the codes, which provided virtual immunity from the Sherman Anti-trust Act, would encourage monopolistic pricing policies and neutralize the Administration's efforts to achieve lower prices for consumers.[22] The tempo of NRA and its administrator, General Hugh Johnson, was another cause for concern. Lippmann saw the purposes of the program jeopardized by what he regarded as undue haste in getting codes accepted.

Striking a new note, Lippmann argued that NRA had originally been conceived as "permissive" in character: in return for compliance with agreed-upon codes, industries were to be permitted to combine, while enjoying immunity from the anti-trust laws. Those industries that elected not to comply were to continue subject to anti-trust laws. Much of the difficulty with NRA, Lippmann held, derived from the unfortunate decision to force compliance instead of permitting industries to choose whether to sign up.[23]

As a corollary to this view, he urged that NRA be reconstructed in such a way as to concentrate on a few large, basic industries. In them competition should be restored and collective bargaining established. If the program failed, the codes could be cancelled and the anti-trust laws again made operative. With respect to the small industries, Lippmann suggested that their codes be regarded as temporary and due to expire shortly.[24]

By the end of 1934 Lippmann was writing NRA off as a costly failure. He held that it had "clogged...the pump which the Administration was trying to prime." But an important benefit had resulted. NRA "so quickly became intolerably complicated and confused that it will be a long time before any one again seriously imagines that the economic life of this nation in all its infinite variety can be planned and directed from Washington." [25] Lippmann rejoiced when Federal Judge Neilds declared the Weirton industry to be intrastate and hence exempt from NRA's guarantees to labor contained in Section 7 (a). In a column titled "A Mighty Blow" Lippmann called the decision a promising step in whittling down NRA's power.[26]

After the Supreme Court invalidated NRA Lippmann's references to it continued in the same vein. He called NRA an act of "midsummer madness," an "almost unmitigated liability," and a vehicle for greatly extending monopoly practices. The President, Lippmann wrote, was indebted to the Supreme Court for rescuing him from the burden of an unworkable NRA.[27]

Climaxing his opposition to programs like NRA with its "centralizing tendencies," Lippmann recommended working through state governments. He admitted that efforts along these lines had been dealt serious blows by the Supreme Court, but he favored this approach nevertheless. At the very least, he thought, his proposal had in its favor greater flexibility and the certainty that it would avoid great national tensions.[28]

LIPPMANN AND THE TENNESSEE VALLEY AUTHORITY

Though few in number, Lippmann's columns on the Tennessee Valley Authority were generally favorable. In his first discussion of the subject he pointed out that certain undertakings of long-range social utility came more properly under public than private auspices. Lippmann did not hesitate to place TVA, with its prospect of long-deferred profits, in this category.

LIPPMANN'S REFERENCES TO TVA (1933-1938)

	Favorable	Unfavorable	Neutral
Number:	3	1	4
Per cent:	37.5	12.5	50

TVA's operational policies, thought Lippmann, had their inspiration in Henry Ford rather than in Karl Marx. Large-volume output at low rates was conceived by the automobile maker and successfully applied by the directors of TVA. The commentator urged businessmen to extend the practice. He also endorsed the concept of decentralized industry, calling it a wholesome trend that should be encouraged.[29]

While approving the principle of TVA, he nevertheless expressed sympathy for the utility operators who, he said, didn't know what territory TVA was planning to invade. Investment in private companies would be paralyzed "if investors do not know from month to month...whether they are to be the next victims of subsidized competition." The Administration, he thought, should state definitely the limits of its intentions along these lines.[30]

The strife among TVA's directors in 1938 inspired several articles in which Lippmann denounced the President's handling of the controversy. Mr. Roosevelt, the columnist insisted, had destroyed the agency's independence by treating Dr. Arthur Morgan, central figure in the dispute, as a personal appointee. By his dismissal of Dr. Morgan, the

President had made of TVA a mere Executive agency. Lippmann predicted that people's confidence in the project would evaporate as a result.[31] But there is nothing in the record to substantiate Lippmann's dreary prediction. There is, on the other hand, impressive evidence that TVA continued to gain in popular approval.

LIPPMANN AND THE NATIONAL LABOR RELATIONS ACT (THE WAGNER ACT)

The tabulation below makes it clear that on the specific piece of legislation known as the Wagner Act Lippmann stood completely opposed. This, however, is not the same as saying he is "anti-labor."

LIPPMANN'S REFERENCES TO THE NATIONAL LABOR
RELATIONS ACT (1934-1938)

	Favorable	Unfavorable	Neutral
Number:	0	12	0
Per cent:	0	100	0

Lippmann's considerable writings are devoid of any statements opposing labor's rights to organize or bargain collectively. There are, on the other hand, many passages affirming these rights. In *Drift and Mastery,* for example, Lippmann described with eloquence and warmth the bond between free labor and free government. He argued, moreover, that strong trade unions promoted stability in industrial relations; that insurrectionary scheming was most likely to occur where workers were despised and weak. "A Key to the Labor Movement," the fifth chapter in *Drift and Mastery,* is a compelling summary of workers' aspirations. Labor theoreticians would be hard put to it to contrive a more persuasive statement of their case in industrial society.

In the early days of NRA Lippmann argued for trade unions that would approximate in bargaining strength the associations of employers.[32] But Senator Robert F. Wagner's proposal to outlaw company unions prompted Lippmann to remark that such a step would mean government fostering of unions and responsibility for their actions.[33] By the middle of 1934 Lippmann's enthusiasm for NRA had cooled. To NRA's famed Section 7 (a), which guaranteed the right of collective bargaining, Lippmann attributed responsibility for labor's restlessness in seeking gains promised but not delivered.[34]

Lippmann's basic objections to the Wagner Act seemed to be that it imposed duties on the government that it could not carry out, and that employers were placed under the absolute obligation to bargain collectively with the representatives of their employees. On the first point, Lippmann insisted that the effort to guarantee collective bargaining on a national scale was an impossible task for a government agency to assume. He predicted that the complexities of administration would be such that paralysis would overtake the organization. "... it is in the last degree foolish to lead labor to think that the Federal government is as omnipotent and as omniscient as this bill requires it to be." As an alternative Lippmann suggested that a new bill be written which would apply to a few large industries. "For these industries government intervention backed by legal compulsion should be limited to the conduct of free elections." [35] This was as far as he would have had the Administration go.

Government, he held, could protect labor's right to organize. But it could never compel an employer to bargain in good faith. He predicted that the Wagner measure must break down "administratively or judicially. If it does not, then it is but a first step in the logical development of general compulsory arbitration.... If the Wagner bill were not so impracticable, it would... be one of the most reactionary measures of our times. If it were not unworkable, it would be dangerous. If it were not a delusion it would be a snare." [36]

In assailing the Wagner measure Lippmann declared that it encouraged labor "to think that the Federal power protects unionization in every town and in every industry in the United States." [37] So far as interstate industry was concerned this was, of course, precisely the intention of the Act. After it had been on the books for over a year he was still denouncing it. It was, he said, "manifestly biased, and the administration of it...incompetent and...prejudiced...." [38]

Legislation designed to hold contracting parties to their agreements was the real remedy to the Wagner measure's shortcomings. This meant, said the columnist, the incorporation of trade unions, their assumption of responsibility for breach of contract, and the disclosure of their financial position.[39]

Lippmann's approach to labor strife had its touch of whimsey. Writing under the title, "The Freshman Class in Collective Bargaining," he advised employers to "remove the class barriers, and begin to acquire the habit of taking lunch with labor leaders and of going to the movies with them...." [40]

Friends of Lippmann regard him as sympathetic to labor and find his record on the Wagner Act "misleading." Basically, they say, he is favorably disposed to unionism. They see no inconsistency in his espousal of labor's rights and his rejection of the Wagner Act.

Labor people, on the other hand, regard the Wagner Act as their Magna Carta. To them it represents the fulfillment of a long struggle for the legally acknowledged right to bargain collectively. The authority of government had finally been brought to bear, in the Wagner Act, as guarantor of that right.

The Wagner Act was a measure in support of which the friends of labor could rise and be counted. Walter Lippmann, champion of the worker's theoretical rights, was not among the measure's partisans. He found fault with this, that, and the other provision of the Act, and stood in firm

opposition to the most important piece of pro-labor legislation ever passed by Congress.

"It has, I think, been clearly established that government must henceforth hold itself consciously responsible
for the maintenance of the standard of life prevailing
among the people. This is, I believe, a new imperative
which takes its place alongside the older imperatives to defend the nation against attack and to preserve domestic
peace." [41]

The above quotation is characteristic of Lippmann's ex-
pressions on the responsibility of government for the economic and social well-being of its people. On this subject
Lippmann has written frequently and with considerable
feeling.

In giving his endorsement to the President's proposed
study on social security in 1934, Lippmann declared,

Underneath all the arguments about unionism, about collective bargaining, about Section 7 (a), and the rest, there is
the profound realization of wage earners that they are the most
exposed, the most vulnerable, the most insecure group in the
nation. Who can deny it? Who can fail to recognize that for
their sakes, as a matter of social justice and social decency, for
the sake of the nation as a whole, the modern state must
assume the obligation to overcome this insecurity? [42]

This was unequivocal language. The columnist's rejection of the dole as a means of sustaining the unemployed
was no less clear. The dole, he maintained, was demoralizing as well as uneconomic. It degraded its recipients and
tended to remove them from the labor market.

To the report of the President's Committee on Economic
Security Lippmann gave hearty approval. He liked especially the provision that a worker, after collecting unemployment insurance for fifteen weeks, was to have the right
to a job on public works where wages would be substan-

tially lower than in private industry. This would serve to make the public employment "distinctly less attractive" than the private.[43]

LIPPMANN'S REFERENCES TO THE SOCIAL
SECURITY PROGRAM (1933-1938)

	Favorable	Unfavorable	Neutral
Number:	5	6	9
Per cent:	25	30	45

Lippmann's enthusiasm for the proposals of the Social Security bill, as the foregoing table suggests, was short-lived. He approved of old-age pensions,[44] but the plan for unemployment insurance stirred doubts. He held that the scheme was full of difficulties, that it would not mitigate the existing or future depressions. He feared that the insurance fund would quickly be emptied and the payments would then be a dole paid by the Treasury.[45]

As an alternative to unemployment insurance Lippmann suggested a great pool of public works that would not compete with private industry. The draining of swamps, reforestation, flood control, highway construction, rural electrification, parks, playgrounds, and housing for the very poor were listed by the columnist as suitable activities. In the same article he endorsed the President's request for four billion dollars to launch a great public-works program. He felt the act signalized "a historic advance towards the security of the people and the preservation of free institutions."[46]

But increasingly Lippmann's emphasis was on the need for retrenchment and balancing the budget. Toward the close of 1935 he began to feel that the worst of the depression was over and that the Federal government should help the states carry out their own relief programs, whether dole or work.[47] As to the states that were too poor to go along on such a plan, he spoke of devising "some method" of helping them.

Commenting on the newly inaugurated social-security

program, he included it among various costly Administration undertakings. That part of the Social Security Act
under which the Federal government made grants he called
"Siphon No. 5." This, he noted, "is not yet operating on a
large scale, but it is generally realized that it has a great
future. Unless past experience means nothing, a pipe has
been laid into the Treasury.... The pressure on Congress
to increase the grants is certain to be persistent and powerful." [48]

Continuing in this vein, he wrote in an article called
"Mr. Roosevelt's Entanglements," that the President had
damaged his position by two ill-conceived programs—"collectivism" and relief expenditures. Lippmann gloomily
forecast a permanent commitment, even after recovery
had been fully achieved, of annual Federal payments of
around two billion dollars to the needy.[49]

Lippmann's conviction as to the need for a social-security
program was tempered by his concern for the budget.
Despite his eloquent pronouncements against the dole, he
seemed ready to see it revived as an economy measure.[50]
The public-works program, which the columnist had called
the most suitable means of caring for the unemployed,
would necessarily have been reduced or eliminated if his
recommendations had been followed.[51]

Yet Lippmann knew the relief problem well. He had
written persuasively and often concerning it. He realized,
of course, that the Federal government had assumed the responsibility for relief only after local efforts had broken
down. He had endorsed the government's assumption of
this burden.[52] That the states were in need of continuing
Federal help was beyond question.[53] Nevertheless he proposed as a solution to what he deemed excessive relief
expenditures, "a drastic reduction of the Federal funds,
which will force the responsibility back upon the localities,
upon families and upon individuals." [54]

But while Lippmann's practical recommendations
meant the emasculation of any genuine program of social
security, he remained, philosophically, in the camp of those

who supported the social-security principle. In 1944 he wrote,

> ... the consequences of unemployment and of economic dislocation have become a recognized national responsibility. The general name for it is Social Security. The prevention of mass unemployment and the regulation of the business cycle are now recognized, except by a disappearing minority, as questions of public policy. The system of free enterprise is therefore no longer what it once was. There is now imposed upon it the obligation to provide reasonably full employment under acceptable conditions of work. This obligation will be enforced by the government, and enterprise is free in so far as it meets the new conditions of its freedom.[55]

The original Murray Full Employment Bill of 1945 had established as the "right" of a citizen "remunerative, regular and full-time employment." This meant, said Lippmann, that a citizen who did not happen to have that kind of employment could, presumably, sue the government for it. The columnist added that this was neither Mr. Roosevelt's nor Mr. Truman's intention. Much better, thought Lippmann, was Senator Robert Taft's proposal to strike out the word "right" and substitute that it was the "policy" of the United States to see that every American had the "opportunity" to gain employment.[56]

Here again Lippmann supported humanitarian principles. But the laws designed to translate those principles into reality did not satisfy him. The net effect of his writing, therefore, was against adoption of basic social legislation.

LIPPMANN AND WAGE-HOUR LEGISLATION

Lippmann strongly opposed the 1937 Connery Bill, designed to effect minimum wages, a limit on hours, and the prohibition of child labor. He found the "whole project of Federal minimum wage laws" to be "misconceived" and incapable of fulfillment. A much better approach, he thought, lay in Federal undertakings to conserve the soil, retire marginal lands, relieve farm tenancy, and develop the TVA. By such measures regional living standards would rise and workers would benefit. "For low wages are not due to chiselers or to the lack of minimum wage laws. They are due to inefficient labor working with inefficient capital under inefficient management." [57]

LIPPMANN'S REFERENCES TO WAGES-AND-HOURS LEGISLATION
(1937-1938)

	Favorable	Unfavorable	Neutral
Number:	0	16	1
Per cent:	0	94	6

The child-labor, hour, and wage provisions of the Connery Bill should, he thought, be separated. A child-labor law should be enacted, to be sure. Maximum hours, however, should be fixed only in those specific industries where bad practices prevailed. Then, "if the Federal government must enter the field of wage fixing" it should pick out a few "sweated industries" and legislate for them. He made a charge that he had often repeated: the Connery measure was the work of amateurs whose knowledge of such legislation was defective. The bill was, moreover, part of the President's plan "to gather together an irresistible power over the economic life of this country and to consolidate that power in the hands of his own following." [58]

Wages-and-hours legislation, he decided, was really a scheme by Northern industry to gain the benefits of an internal protective tariff.[59] This, he said, explained the support of Senator Henry Cabot Lodge, Republican from Massachusetts. Back of the legislation, said the columnist, were two groups: "reactionaries, who know just what it really means and ... Northern reformers who have never been in the South." With undeniable justice he showed that the South needed, and in equity deserved, an equalization of railroad rates, credit facilities, and interest rates.[60]

Lippmann's charge that Northern manufacturers saw selfish advantage in the lifting of Southern wage levels was undoubtedly true. But the potential benefit of this legislation to large groups of exploited laborers was irrefutable.

To the wretchedly underpaid Southern worker Lippmann offered the prospect of improved conditions when the region was rehabilitated. This was remote, even if certain. The columnist's insistence that the law would undermine Southern industry proved to be one of his worst guesses. Most progressives supported the wages-and-hours legislation for the immediate, important gains it promised —and achieved.

While there is much to be said for an unhurried and philosophical approach to social reform, a point is reached beyond which continued insistence on perfection means frustration and defeat. Lippmann's inability to accept most New Deal measures in their entirety meant that in effect he ranged himself with the enemies of this legislation. In virtually every case he approved of the principle while rejecting its legislative embodiment. If his arguments had convinced a majority of legislators, the New Deal would at best have added up to an innocuous set of half-measures.

CHAPTER SIX

LIPPMANN AS PREDICTOR:
NATIONAL AND INTERNATIONAL AFFAIRS

WHEN THE WHOLE OF LIPPMANN'S WRITTEN OUTPUT is considered, the singular fact emerges that he has done relatively little predicting. The temptation to prophesy is undoubtedly strong in column writers who, because of the nature of their work, must inevitably think of themselves as possessing oracular powers. If the record of other columnists in this respect is used as a basis, Lippmann's position appears unique. For he has, as a rule, been content to base his observations and theories on day-to-day developments. As a general practice he has, in the true spirit of scholarship, made a searching examination of the relevant data and then drawn his conclusions. His discussion of foreign affairs, as this chapter will show, has the same sober, judicious quality as his analysis of domestic problems.

Lippmann has never sought to entertain, titillate, or shock his readers by fanciful interpretations. Only occasionally has he ventured to forecast future trends. These prognostications are worthy of examination not because they establish Lippmann as either a good guesser or a poor one, but because they afford insight into the trends of his thinking—and perhaps of his hopes.

The youthful Lippmann, in one of his earliest published predictions, thought that the Constitution was "decadent." He felt the same about such concepts as the "Sanctity of Private Property, Vested Rights, [and] Competition the

Life of Trade...." He concluded that "the early maxims of capitalism are doomed."[1]

Another of his early predictions appeared in *Drift and Mastery*. Here Lippmann anticipated that the consumer would become the determining factor in the nation's economy, transcending in importance both labor and capital. "With the consumer awake, neither the worker nor the employer can use politics for his special interest." He found the consumers using government to impose on business "a maximum of quality and a minimum of cost." Women, having once received the franchise, would insure that the consumer became "the real master of the political situation."[2] Businessmen would eventually discover that consumers would not tolerate "unreasonable" profits.[3] The fate of the 1934 Tugwell Pure Food Bill, done to death by the drug and newspaper lobbies, and of efforts to enforce grade labelling of foods suggests that the consumer's influence has been progressively reduced rather than increased. The upward spiralling of prices following the removal of World War II controls, further discounts Lippmann's cheery view.

In *Drift and Mastery*, too, he saw the eclipse of the profiteer. Leaders of business, he argued, were becoming increasingly conscious of their responsibilities to the public. This was a "dim recognition that the motives in business are undergoing a revolution."[4] The new group of professional managers, in Lippmann's view, stood "outside the higgling of the market" and were not activated by the profit motive.

He predicted the development of a great corps of scientifically trained directors who would administer their industries with the same kind of disinterested competence as the most gifted leaders in the professions. To such men mere accumulation was of secondary importance. Their basic interest lay in the work itself.[5]

Lippmann saw the railways coming under government control; stockholding in this industry was "in the last stages of decay." While a "vast amount" of private business would continue, the big, staple industries were likely to go the way of publicly owned railroads. "Private property," he ventured to say, "will melt away...." [6]

The trusts, Lippmann said in the same volume, "are organizing private property out of existence, are altering its nature so radically that very little remains but the title and the ancient theory." [7] But he had a unique conception of "private" as against "public" property: a corporation that was under the ostensible direction of salaried managers and whose stock was widely held, had the attributes of a "public" enterprise.

... when a corporation has become really great, the old distinction between public and private interest becomes very dim. I think it is destined largely to disappear. It is difficult even to-day to say whether the great railways, the General Electric Company, the United States Steel Corporation, the bigger insurance companies and banks are public or private institutions. [8]

An industry, because it affected large numbers of people, lost its private character and became "public." [9] Lippmann ignored the critical question of whether the enterprise was operated for private profit.

He proceeded from this point to predict that in the future the leaders of big business would "retire" from money-making before accepting top positions. Young men aspiring to important executive posts would, before taking such jobs, arrange their private affairs so that they could live on their salaries and not be suspected of trying to make money. "For, in the future, to make a fortune will be considered as improper for the head of a big business as for the President of the United States or the mayor of a city." [10]

If Lippmann's prediction about a "revolution" in businessmen's motives contains a strong element of fantasy, his prophecies in other areas have been better sustained by events. He pointed out long before the days of fascism that a great mass of unemployed, propertyless citizens were a ready tool for the forces of reaction. Even the socialists, he noted, despaired of the depressed slum-dwellers. For they were "the most easily led, the most easily fooled, and the most easily corrupted." [11] He noted later that the uniting of the plutocracy and the proletariat was a characteristic pattern in fascist countries. [12] From this point he proceeded to recommend steps for raising the proletariat to a "middle condition," urging that they be endowed with sufficient property to give them a vested interest in a secure, stable society. [13]

Less accurate was Lippmann's prediction as to where fascism might develop. He maintained that industrialized countries operated under a mechanism so intricate that they could not be managed from any central point by a single brain or cabinet of brains. Lippmann's conclusion was perhaps inevitable: "Here is the essential reason why bolshevism and fascism are, as we say, un-American. They are no less un-Belgian, un-German, un-English. For they are un-industrial." [14]

Not long after Lippmann wrote these words Adolph Hitler directed from Berlin the construction of a war machine that speedily crushed most of Europe. The extension by the Nazis of Draconian rule over their subjects does not appear to have been impeded by the advanced state of German industry. On the contrary, the Nazis utilized every technological advance in building and securing their system of terror.

Disturbing, also, was Lippmann's assertion that fascism was "un-American" and "un-English." He suggested thereby that these countries enjoyed an inherent immunity from fascism. But given a certain combination of economic, political, and social conditions fascism, by whatever name it is known, is, of course, possible in any country. To believe that our country was necessarily secure from fascism was to be unrealistic in the highest degree. Yet this was Lippmann's published view as late as 1929.

Nor did Lippmann accurately prophesy the future of fascism in Germany. Four months after Hitler came to power Lippmann declared that Nazism would evaporate if all the Germans had jobs.[15] They did, of course, eventually obtain jobs—under a firmly entrenched Nazi regime.

In the days before Warren G. Harding became President, Lippmann wrote an essay called "An Anticipation of Harding." In it he forecast with considerable accuracy what Harding would be like. "The Grand Dukes have chosen their weak Tsar in order to increase the power of the Grand Dukes," he wrote.[16] The article was a plea for an Executive who would not shrink from exercising leadership.

Lippmann's predictions on the gold standard swung from one extreme to the other. Late in 1932 he wrote that by defending the gold standard the United States had successfully survived the "culminating crisis of the depression." He maintained, oddly, that our support of gold had "arrested the most powerful deflationary force still operating in the world."[17] At least twice thereafter he denounced talk of abandoning the gold standard and recited the evils that would follow such a move.[18] But within three weeks of his most recent jeremiad he found it possible to applaud our departure from gold. He saw hoarding ended, bank assets becoming liquid, and the beginnings of a needed rise in prices.[19] Whereas he had opposed leaving gold because of the danger of inflation, he now urged the government to take bold steps to promote "controlled" inflation. He recommended that the government, the Federal Reserve system, banks, and industries work together to expand the currency and enlarge purchasing power. He included increased relief, public works, and government loans to industry as basic parts of the program.[20]

Thereby Lippmann reversed himself on the gold standard, on inflation, and on public works. But with candor he said, "...these are times when men must be willing to accept the conclusions of the evidence as they see it, and be ready to take the risks of stating their conclusions."[21] He had come, suddenly, to believe that the closing of the banks and government retrenchment, among other factors, had helped drive down prices. Accordingly, he took the honorable—and inevitable—position of encouraging inflation.

Lippmann doubted that Governor Franklin D. Roosevelt had the necessary qualifications for the Presidency. The columnist interpreted Roosevelt's primary-election difficulties in Pennsylvania and Massachusetts as proof that his nomination would "disunite and disperse" any support the Party might have lined up. Lippmann maintained that results in the two states offered confirmation "by the urban masses of the East" that Roosevelt was unfit for the Presidency.[22] Shortly after, in an article titled "The Deflation of Franklin Roosevelt," the columnist declared that if the Governor received the 1932 Presidential nomination he would be defeated, "unless this is a year when any Democrat can be elected...." Lippmann predicted that Roosevelt's "inherent weaknesses" would quickly show up during the campaign. Roosevelt did not have a "good enough grasp of issues nor the power of quick and firm decision to withstand the withering fire which the Republicans would subject him to." [23]

It has been shown in Chapter V that Lippmann was for the most part opposed to NRA. But his original prediction was that NRA was "almost certain to mark a permanent and basic change in industrial control." He had recommended that public opinion adjust itself to the reality of this "new industrial order." [24] But when he changed his mind about NRA he condemned the plan without equivocation: the President's "collectivism," as exemplified by NRA, AAA, and the Guffey Coal Act, was contrary to the American tradition, and the American people would not be induced to change their Constitution to allow such a development; the President's relief program threatened that we would be "permanently committed, even with full recovery," to gigantic payments to the needy.[25]

In his occasional predictions about the ending of the depression Lippmann was excessively optimistic. In 1935 he thought that Mr. Roosevelt should relinquish to Congress the extensive powers he had been given to achieve recovery; the battle was over.[26] A year later he urged ade-

quate measures to regulate "the coming boom," which he
felt was so close that no time could be lost in preparing for
it.[27]

In a broadcast of June 28, 1936 he pronounced the New
Deal dead. Recovery had been achieved in spite of Mr.
Roosevelt's program, which the Supreme Court had ob-
literated. Any sentiment for amending the Constitution
had been dissipated by improved economic conditions.[28]

The Democrats faced disaster, said Lippmann, unless
they abandoned what he called centralized control of
economic policies. Citing the unhappy precedent of the
Eighteenth Amendment, he predicted that Federal regulation of prices, wages, and working conditions would revive
the noisome evils associated with Federal Prohibition.[29]

Though he favored the candidacy of Alf Landon, Lippmann at no time predicted that his choice would win. He
seems to have regarded the President's re-election as certain.
This may be inferred from Lippmann's recommendation
that the voters substantially increase the Republican rep-
resentation in the House as a means of checking Roosevelt. The columnist declared that "another Democratic
landslide" would be a calamity for the President, the Party,
and the country. Mr. Roosevelt was not likely to grow in
"judgment" or "magnanimity" after a great popular victory; the Democratic Party would become increasingly a
"sectional and class organization," and the country would
be deprived of a virile opposition to Administration
policies.[30]

Late in 1939, when third-term talk was rife, *Time* discussed Lippmann's views on the subject in almost four
columns. After a detailed description of the process by
which he reached his conclusions, *Time* said that "De-
tective Lippmann" was convinced that Mr. Roosevelt
would renounce a third term.[31]

Senator Wagner's 1934 proposal to outlaw company
unions drew a sharp reply from Lippmann. Such a move,
he said, would put the government in the position of
"fostering" unions and would make it "responsible" for

the unions' behavior. Other consequences he foresaw were "labor monopolies" and compulsory arbitration.[32]

At least twice before the founding of the Congress of Industrial Organizations Lippmann forecast the development of new-type unions.[33] He thought the American Federation of Labor unequal to the demands engendered by Section 7 (a) of NRA. The new unions, he correctly anticipated, would be industry-wide in character. With less accuracy, he pronounced the craft unions doomed.[34]

The National Labor Relations Act inspired some of Lippmann's least successful predictions. He argued that according to the Wagner Act employers were compelled to bargain in good faith. This he termed a "legal monstrosity" that could not be enforced. For while government could protect the workers' right to organize, it could never require an employer to negotiate "in good faith." Compulsion, he concluded, was incompatible with collective bargaining and would never work.[35]

Lippmann doubted that the Wagner Act would be sustained by the courts. But if it were, he predicted a dark future for it: "interminable and inconclusive litigation and dispute," and eventual nullification either by the courts or by the "sheer difficulties of administration."[36]

The columnist's opposition seems to have been inspired in part by semantics. Not only were "bargaining in good faith" and "compulsion" mutually exclusive terms, but the language of the Wagner bill was insufficiently precise. It set up "undefined rights" which would have to be settled by the courts. The measure, moreover, would lead labor to think that unionization would be everywhere protected by the Federal government. He argued, also, that the bill "distorted" the election device "by the untrue assumption that elections will show a clear majority." He was concerned that in some cases workers' representatives might be elected by a mere plurality instead of a majority.[37] The Wagner Act, if it survived the court tests and didn't break down administratively, would eventuate in compulsory arbitration. Therefore, if the measure were not so "impracticable," it would be "one of the most reactionary measures of our times." [38]

It is not to be wondered at that Lippmann opposed the 1948 candidacy of Harry S. Truman. The President's espousal of the Wagner Act and the rest of the New Deal, coupled with what Lippmann called his proved incompetence, made Mr. Truman an impossible candidate. Along with almost everybody else, Lippmann predicted the President's defeat. The Democratic Party, said the columnist, was in receivership. It needed only to be commended to "caretakers" who presumably would nurse it along during Thomas E. Dewey's Presidency.

Mr. Truman's startling victory and the vigorous resurgence of his party embarrassed Lippmann no less than the other experts. He confessed his error and, strangely, attributed the Truman victory to the power of the Roosevelt New Deal. Twelve years earlier Lippmann had concluded that the New Deal was dead.

In the field of foreign affairs, to a greater degree than on domestic issues, Lippmann has reversed himself on his early predictions and hopes. From a youthful advocate of collective security—League of Nations style—he has become, in the words of a friend, "a somewhat recent convert to power politics." The introduction to Lippmann's *U.S. Foreign Policy: Shield of the Republic* [39] contains a revealing confession of previous error. Here he candidly admitted that he had discarded many of his old beliefs. His present views, he added, were the distillation of thirty years of thinking and writing on the subject of our foreign affairs. He chided himself for having failed to understand the dynamics of foreign policy in the past, mentioning as an example his support for the "exorbitant folly" of the Washington Disarmament Conference of 1921-22. Concerning that episode, he added, "I am ashamed, all the more so because I had no excuse for not knowing better." [40]

Lippmann has always opposd a policy of isolation for this country. He has consistently advocated that the United States assume active leadership in international affairs.

Such a rôle, he long ago noted, would be a radical departure for us, for we loved the "irresponsibility" of isolation. But the realities of international affairs demanded action, not passivity. "Real isolation has, in fact, become a myth, and our only choice is between being the passive victim of international disorder and resolving to be an active leader in ending it." [41]

Early in his writing career Lippmann declared categorically that the primary cause for wars was the existence of weak, backward areas in Asia, Africa, the Balkans, and Central and South America. These rich territories invited exploitation by competing adventurers, and wars resulted.[42] The way to end conflict was for international commissions to take control of these undeveloped lands and thereby render them inaccessible to private exploiters. The experience gained by international agencies in such activities would facilitate co-operation in other spheres; the result would be a wholesome reduction of national sovereignty.

Here he was forecasting the trusteeship idea, though his belief that it contained the cure for wars was unduly optimistic. With some naivete he declared that if international agencies controlled undeveloped areas, individual capitalists could be deterred from calling on their home governments for support. The governments, he added, might help their nationals by "diplomatic argument" but never by military intervention.[43]

Because of his identification with the Wilson Administration, and his writings about the wartime President, Lippmann was known as a "Wilson man." [44] Lippmann had helped to formulate the Fourteen Points. Their official interpretation was almost entirely his own work. With certain reservations he had approved the League of Nations, professing to see in it a great agency for remaking the world.[45] He had thought that the coalition of powers in World War I was the beginning of international federation and a hopeful lessening of national sovereignty.[46]

Recently, however, Lippmann repudiated his early predictions of a Wilsonian world. In his 1944 publication,

U.S. War Aims, he rejected Wilsonian principles point by point, arguing that they spelled self-emasculation for modern nations. Wilson's League, according to Lippmann, was designed to create "a world state under the sovereignty of mankind." [47] If such an organization had really been possible Wilson's ideals of "military and diplomatic disarmament and of self-determination" would have been appropriate.[48] But in our world, Lippmann argued, such principles were the ultimate folly. Proof of this became evident in the 1930's when the democracies, reduced almost to impotence by disarmament and pacifism, helplessly watched the Nazi tyrants climb to power. Almost too late the free countries were rescued from their disastrous policies.

Wilson's ideal of self-determination, or the right of each people to create a separate nation, was likewise mistaken, for it meant the continous splintering of states. Minorities might form endlessly within other minorities until chaos prevailed. Lippmann supported his argument by citing Hitler's use of the self-determination principle. In Austria, Czechoslovakia, Poland, Belgium, the Ukraine, the Caucasus, in Brazil, and among the Arabs, the Nazi dictator had used this policy as a weapon of aggrandizement.[49] Self-determination, Lippmann insisted, was a denial of the civilized ideal that diverse peoples might enjoy liberty and security under any nation's laws.

Wilson's doctrines originated in a "love of liberty and of justice," and were "inspired by a righteous compassion." But they were so badly attuned to the realities of modern society that they precipitated disorder and struggle. Thus Wilson's projected disarmament meant, in Lippmann's view, that a nation would be obliged to wait passively until the aggressor had sprung his attack.[50]

A general world organization that had for its purpose to prevent war could not succeed, said Lippmann.[51] Issues of war and peace were not best handled in a public forum. They must be decided "in quiet and in confidence by those who have the responsibility because they have the power."

To ventilate such matters in open debate was to exacerbate feelings and insure failure.

An international society should not be burdened with a task it could not fulfill: the prevention of war. There was, nevertheless, a legitimate function for a world organization: the cultivation of "the arts of peace." The non-political departments of the League of Nations afforded a worthy model. Among appropriate fields of endeavor were the combating of disease, poverty, and ignorance; the interchange of cultural achievements, and the development of international trade.[52]

The only way to preserve world order was to transform the wartime "nuclear alliance" of the United States, Great Britain, Russia, and China into regional systems: the Atlantic Community, the Russian Orbit, the Chinese Orbit, and Indian and Moslem communities.[53] Each of these configurations of states, he said, represented a natural affinity from the standpoint of defense. Each would have the responsibility for preserving a stable community and, moreover, each would be endowed with the instruments to make its will effective. Small states and neutral states would have to find places within the larger areas of which they were strategic parts.[54] These large groups would then constitute a world society capable of maintaining peace for an indefinite period.

Lippmann did not object to a world order as such. He maintained, however, that a universal organization made up of sixty or more individual nations simply could not keep the peace. Though he put forward this idea too recently to be judged, most authorities would agree that events are confirming Lippmann's melancholy prediction.

It is worth noting that Lippmann's proposals in *U.S. War Aims* were predicated on an armed world. Great regional groupings of nations would be in a kind of equilibrium with respect to each other. Peace, he thought, would be assured under these conditions, because the most provocative forms of "interference and intervention" would not exist in a world of stable communities.[55]

Most significant, perhaps, was the fact that his proposals were free of any suggestion for reducing national sovereignty. Whereas he had once looked toward the minimization of this force, he now took a more cynical—perhaps more realistic—view of the problem. If it were possible to keep the peace, massed strength alone could do it. Lippmann had indeed been converted to power politics.

As relations between Russia and the United States became more tense in the months following World War II, Lippmann wrote a series of columns, later published in book form, called *The Cold War*.[56] The essence of his argument was that there could be no peace in Europe until all armies of liberation were withdrawn. If his proposals were followed, European rehabilitation could begin in earnest. The Truman Doctrine, designed to "contain" Soviet communism, was certain to fail and to insure the destruction of the United Nations as well. The United States had embarked on a herculean task of propping up a motley array of ruling groups in the vain hope that they would form dependable links in a chain to limit communist expansion. We were heading, he said, into a costly disaster.

United States support for a "truncated" German national state in the western zones was, said Lippmann, playing into Russian hands. The Soviets would thereby acquire the power to complete German territorial unity. In return for suitable concessions Russia might well negotiate with an "independent" Germany of our own creation. Lippmann pleaded that we avoid such a tragic conclusion to our cold war.

The Atlantic Pact of 1949 had Lippmann's firm support. He approved the arming of member nations as an earnest of America's determination to stand with them in case any was assaulted.

In an article called "The Russian-American War," published in *Atlantic* in July, 1949, Lippmann epitomized his views on our relations with the Soviet Union. Advocates of a quick, decisive air attack on Russia, he said, are urging America to commit suicide. For the history of the

Soviet regime shows that the demolition of its physical resources must strengthen, not weaken its determination to survive. Communism, in short, is here to stay.

Our strategy, in these circumstances, should be twofold: to make known that we will tolerate no incursions into Atlantic Pact territories; and to assure the Russians that we plot no aggressive action against them. We would then achieve a kind of peace by pressure. While remaining scrupulously faithful to our Atlantic Pact commitments, we would nevertheless recognize the Russians' pre-eminent position in their own sphere.

In recent articles Lippmann insisted that the correctness of his position was established by two tremendous events: the achievement by the Russians of anatomic explosion, and the debacle in the Far East. The "phantom policy" of trying to "contain" the Soviets had blown away, he said. Now there was no alternative to negotiating a balance-of-power settlement.

An increasingly cynical Lippmann declared, in a recent address, that rivalry, strife, and conflict "among states, communities, and factions is the normal condition of mankind." But, he added, American foreign policy has always refused to recognize this basic fact. We have been dominated by the belief that international struggle is wrong, or abnormal, or transitory. When nations have warred our first reaction was to try to be neutral. Then we joined the crusade to eliminate the chief troublemaker. Having defeated him in a costly war, we sponsored a universal society to prevent future wars. But absolute stability in the world has not, and never will be achieved.

It is the task of diplomacy, said Lippmann, to compose differences between nations, to relieve tensions, to give and to take without engaging in war. The choice must not be total peace or total war. The first, he said, is impossible because it ignores basic human impulses; the second would mean defeat for victor and vanquished alike. But somewhere between them a way of life can be worked out. Power and compromise, skillfully employed, are the essentials for success. Our goal should be not to end rivalry, but rather to prevent it from developing into savage, universal conflict.[57] If Lippmann is right we may achieve not peace, but a truce.

Because he has held his predictions firmly in check, Lippmann has been spared the embarrassment that attends bad guesses. While one of his friends laughingly refers to him as "a merry little repudiator," his record, nevertheless, is relatively good. His predictions, whether of foreign or domestic events, have been infrequent, restrained, and carefully considered. In his earlier years they had a starry-eyed quality. More recently they have been earthbound, dealing more with the world as it is than as he would like it to be.

Readers hunting for sensations or the pronouncements of a crystal-gazer have had to turn elsewhere for satisfaction. Lippmann has, as the next chapter shows, written for the solid section of the American community.

CHAPTER SEVEN

TO WHOM DOES LIPPMANN APPEAL?

I̶N A LONG LITERARY CAREER WALTER LIPPMANN HAS championed and opposed many issues, parties, and men. He has, in his writing, appealed to different groups at different times. With the passing years, of course, came altered judgments and new perspectives. On certain matters, however, he has adhered rather steadily to positions taken early in his professional life.

Among those toward whom Lippmann has been generally friendly have been America's industrial leaders. In his first book, published in 1913, Lippmann wrote about the "higher motives" of businessmen. He made an ardent plea that business be regarded as something more than a vulgar search for profits. "Instead of telling businessmen not to be greedy, we should tell them to be industrial statesmen, applied scientists, and members of a craft." Scientifically trained businessmen would regard production "as a creative art instead of as a brute exploitation." Eventually we would have a people "released from a stupid fixation upon the silly little ideals of accumulating dollars and filling their neighbor's eye." [1]

In his desire to impute loftier aims to businessmen, Lippmann implied that the public was somehow ungenerous in its view; that a more trusting attitude by the people would inspire better behavior by business. He found big businessmen thinking seriously about their "responsibilities" and their "stewardship." The motives in business, he thought, were being thoroughly revised in the public interest.[2]

It must be remembered that Lippmann had had more than a layman's acquaintance with the muckraking movement. As assistant to Lincoln Steffens he had studied at first hand the depredations of corrupt business in the early years of the twentieth century. But in his *Drift* and *Mastery,* which appeared in 1914, he treated the subject of muckraking in cavalier fashion. He said that to enumerate the kinds of graft that had recently been exposed was a suitable task for "a few German scholars, young and in perfect health," who might be imported for the purpose. But any such picture, he said, would be "false and inept." [3] The important inference to be drawn from the concentrated interest in business behavior, he thought, was that new and higher incentives were at work. "Muckraking is full of the voices of the beaten, of the bewildered.... It has pointed to a revolution in business motives; it has hinted at the emerging power of labor and the consumer...." Muckraking was, so to speak, a mere episode on the march forward, "more of an effect than a sign of leadership." He found it "impossible to say that muckraking was either progressive or reactionary in its tendency." [4]

That he could take such a disinterested attitude toward muckraking suggests that he was uncommonly well disposed toward businessmen. It is noteworthy that these tolerant views appeared in his two books which are most critical of the existing economic order. For *Preface to Politics* and *Drift and Mastery* represent the adult Lippmann furthest to the left. In the second work, especially, he inveighed against the cruelty of industry and made out a compelling case for trade unionism. At the same time he found it possible to give a highly idealized account of the businessman.[5]

In an equivocal article that appeared during the depression [6] Lippmann cited the grievances of the American people against certain businessmen: they had enriched themselves by unethical means; they had taken advantage of inside tips; they had served themselves instead of their shareholders. For their selfishness such businessmen were properly held in low repute. But, he continued, the future was bright, for a new concept of the industrialist was bound to come. Lippmann proceeded to elaborate his view that capitalists were regarding their responsibilities like top civil officers. He still seems to feel that "the tendency" exists for businessmen to become "industrial statesmen"; that motives of prestige and power count more with well-paid executives than profit.

Lippmann's writing is not without its criticism of business practices. His earliest works were in part an arraignment of private industry.[7] In the 1932 campaign he condemned the Republican Party repeatedly for bringing the country to its then unhappy position.[8] In the first two years of the New Deal Lippmann reaffirmed his opposition to Republican policies. He denounced the corporations which during the depression had kept their prices high and their production down.[9] He assailed Old Guard Republicanism for having fostered the twin evils of monopoly and high tariffs. He held that because big business had insisted on excessively high prices at home and an end to competition from abroad our economy was being strangled.[10] He condemned the holding company in principle.[11]

Most of Lippmann's discussions of economic affairs, however, have been calculated to bring comfort to business. As has been indicated, even the writing that represented the high-water mark of his radicalism was not without its reassurances to industry. While the depression was at its worst, the columnist said that if recovery were to be achieved the government would have to encourage capitalists, big and little, to invest for profit. "They will not do it to earn a Blue Eagle. They will not do it for patriotism's sake or as an act of public service. They will do it because they see a chance to make money. This is the capitalist system. That is the way it works."[12] Lippmann seemed to have forgotten here his attribution of "higher motives" to businessmen. In this same period, moreover, he justified the "very great inheritance" of John D. Rockfeller, Jr., who, according to Lippmann, regarded it "as a trust to be administered for the public benefit." [13] This was in sharp contrast to the opinion he had held back in his *New Republic* days.[14]

In *Drift and Mastery* Lippmann seemed to feel that such industries as railroads, steel, oil, lumber, and coal were likely to be taken over "by government commissions [and] by developing labor unions." [15] But twenty years later, in *Method of Freedom*, he stood squarely for the sanctity of private property, even maintaining that "the only dependable foundation of personal liberty is the personal economic security of private property." [16]

In this same volume Lippmann developed the thesis that a society was secure to the extent that it had a great property-owning middle class. He saw only danger in the existence of a large proletariat. The "middle condition," with private property extensively held, was the ideal. He then proceeded to glorify the middle class, lauding their supposed virtues, and professing to see in them the fulfillment of society's legitimate aspirations. They stood for peace and order; they could be counted on to conduct the public business "cooly and prosaically"; they were not the kind to seek adventure "in the streets" nor would they be readily affected by "the contagious fevers of huddled and amorphous crowds."

Lippmann was not disturbed by the charge that the middle class were "bourgeois and dull," that they "dislike what is too clever and too original." For they had hold of the essence of liberty and they could be counted on to cling to it stubbornly.[17] Lippmann has not often extolled mediocrity in this way.

In solving the problem of proletarian insecurity, Lippmann made it clear that he intended no attack on plutocratic wealth. Taking from the rich and giving to the poor would solve nothing and would, in fact, disrupt the economy. Proletarianism had to be broken up by giving the poor a vested interest in society, by seeing to it that they acquired property.[18]

On the subject of taxation Lippmann's views were likewise inoffensive to businessmen. Before President-elect Franklin D. Roosevelt took office, the columnist criticized him for opposing the sales tax. The alternative, income taxes, would have to be levied against the poor and middle classes, for in Lippmann's view not much more could be taken from the rich.[19] Writing some time later, he agreed with the President's proposal to curb excessive individual net incomes by taxes. But he accused Mr. Roosevelt of undue haste in trying to put through his "soak-the-rich" tax bill. The President, Lippmann urged in 1935, should stop acting as though an emergency still existed.[20] Furthermore, Mr. Roosevelt should have imposed taxes, however small, on the low-income groups, to promote a sense of "responsibility" among them.[21] In this recurring emphasis on the desirability of laying direct taxes on small incomes,[22] and in his clearly expressed hostility to mounting Federal expenditures, Lippmann paralleled the opinions of businessmen.[23]

Though he had taken a stand against holding companies,[24] he criticized the government's efforts to break them up. He condemned the "death sentence" with no less vigor than did the utility companies themselves.[25] The government, he felt, had not taken into account that the utilities were relatively new industries, whose bizarre financial practices might perhaps be attributed to their pioneering spirit.[26] A more charitable attitude is hard to imagine.

Elsewhere it has been shown that Lippmann's eloquent advocacy of a public-works program was neutralized by his concern for the expenditures involved.[27] Wages on these public works, he said, should be sufficient to insure "a bare but self-respecting existence...."[28] He did not explain how a "bare" existence could also be "self-respecting."

In *Good Society* Lippmann denounced monopoly, arguing that it represented a serious restriction on the operation of the market economy. Every monopoly, he added, existed by virtue of some kind of legal privilege. His remedy, discussed in Chapter III, was to "change the law." It is doubtful whether this proposal alienated the columnist's monopoly-minded followers.

Lippmann's views on "collectivism" and economic planning have been described in Chapters III and V. In *Method of Freedom* he championed a "free collectivism" or "compensated" economy, in which the government would constitute a balance wheel in the private-enterprise system. Under this plan the government would stand ready at all times to bring into play a variety of controls capable of offsetting the countless private transactions of our capitalist organization.[29]

But about the middle of 1935 his articles began to show a growing opposition to "collectivism" and economic planning. These views received their fullest exposition in *Good Society,* published in 1937, and which, according to the author, he had started to write four years earlier.[30] Among those to whom Lippmann acknowledged his indebtedness was "Professor F. von Hayek, whose critique of planned economy has brought a new understanding of the whole problem of collectivism...."[31] Hayek later became celebrated for his attack on government planning that appeared under the title *The Road to Serfdom.*

Lippmann's denunciation of collectivism, not unwelcome to conservative readers, was sweeping and inclusive. He even maintained that the "gradual collectivism" of the democratic states was a negation of true liberalism and a forerunner of totalitarian collectivism. He argued that it was impossible to plan successfully for whole nations unless they were poor or at war.[32] In a free and rich society, he said, planning obstructed the functioning of the market, the means by which modern nations had achieved both liberty and wealth.

Detailed analysis has already been given in Chapters IV and V on how Lippmann felt about specific pieces of

New Deal legislation and about Mr. Roosevelt as President. It need only be mentioned here that he wrote more unfavorable than favorable columns in every case but one (TVA); and that he wrote more unfavorable than neutral columns in every case but two (TVA and Social Security).

To be sure, Lippmann criticized Hoover, especially in the months before the 1932 election,[33] and even occasionally thereafter.[34] But several pre-election and most of the post-election references to Hoover were favorable.[35] Nor did the Republican Party escape attack.[36] But the evidence documenting Lippmann's basic hostility to the New Deal is irrefutable. And his support of Landon in the 1936 election may be taken as a measure of exculpation for the Republican Party, in spite of the harsh statements the columnist had sometimes made about it.

Though Lippmann may have twitted the Old Guard, he struck telling blows at the New Deal. His attacks on what he called "collectivism" were designed to cut the ground from under the Roosevelt reform program; conservatives could not fail to take heart. At the same time he innocently believed that monopoly could be ended by "changing the law." His suggestion that monopolists would one day see that they were obstructing the free operation of the market [37] must have disturbed them but mildly. As important a witness as Wendell Berge, former Assistant Attorney-General of the United States has meanwhile testified that "...the concentration of economic power in this country is increasing above any previous crest of monopoly in our history....The monopoly problem is today more serious than at any time since the passage of the Sherman Act." [38]

To the New Dealers who were trying to meet head-on the challenge of mass unemployment and insecurity, Lippmann's strictures against "collectivism" seemed irrelevant. To his protestations that he was championing the "true" liberalism they could only feel that his preachments added up to reaction. He was denounced as an unwitting instrument of fascism [39] and an apologist for the rich.[40]

Among the ideas for which Walter Lippmann is most widely known are those dealing with public opinion. His notion of the people's rôle in national affairs appealed to that minority who distrusted popular processes of government. In books and articles he belittled the importance of public opinion and the validity of majority rule.

In *Public Opinion*, which appeared in 1922, he ridiculed the idea of the "omnicompetent" citizen who could decide intelligently on the great issues of the time. In Jefferson's day, when society was relatively simple and a village economy prevailed, it was possible, he said, for the public to have valid opinions on a variety of questions.[41] But in our generation it was self-deception to believe that a citizen could understand even the tiniest part of the problems demanding solution.

Stereotypes, he held, were an important part of one's thought processes. Though they had their uses they necessarily set limits to man's perception. Every idea that entered a person's head was first filtered through his particular bundle of stereotypes. Agreement as to "facts" became almost impossible as a result. Man's understanding of events depended on his particular mind-images. "Neither justice, nor mercy, nor truth, enter into such a judgment, for the judgment has preceded the evidence."[42]

Nor could the newspapers be counted on to supply the intelligence on which dependable judgments could be based. For at best the press recorded a selected number of events seen through the eyes of a reporter. The press was "like the beam of a searchlight that moves restlessly about, bringing one episode and then another out of darkness into vision. Men cannot do the work of the world by this light alone. They cannot govern society by episodes, incidents, and eruptions."[43] To expect the press to provide impartial and complete coverage of the numberless occurrences of the day was to impose on it an impossible burden.

A solution to the dilemma lay in the development of bureaus of intelligence. These agencies would be staffed with experts who had not "policies," but the skill to isolate facts and offer them as a basis for making judgments.[44] The precedents for this approach Lippmann found in the practice of executives to utilize the services of "statisticians, accountants, auditors, industrial counsellors...scientific managers, [and] personnel administrators...." [45] Lippmann professed to see great possibilities in this scheme. Here at last was a device for making meaningful the "unseen environment." Factfinders had a valid rôle to perform; they alone were capable of handling the tools that social science had made available.

The general citizenry had neither the time, the ability, nor the inclination to inform itself on important questions. Society was too complex, the power of stereotypes too great, man's immediate environment too dominant. Our only hope lay in boards of experts who could distill the evidence and offer the residue of facts.

In *Phantom Public,* a 1925 publication dealing with the same subject, Lippmann constricted even further the scope of public opinion. He denied that the mere "compounding of individual ignorances in masses of people can produce a continuous directing force in public affairs." [46] It was beyond the capacity of human beings to deal with the substance of questions. They were not able to evaluate the evidence on which decisions had to be based. All they could be expected to do was to determine whether the principals in a controversy were behaving according to settled rules. Chapters Eight to Twelve of this volume contained his formula for ascertaining whether appropriate rules were being observed. Lippmann seemed to have despaired even of the "experts" as a force for enlightenment. He had decided that their findings were not sufficiently interesting to engage the attention of the public; besides, there were too many other demands on the citizens' time.[47]

Lippmann rejected the idea that the people governed. Instead, he argued, they periodically mobilized and intervened in public affairs. Their preferences, as expressed in elections, were not indicative of their basic convictions, but were usually a profession of support for one of several aspirants for office.[48] The issues involved were generally too numerous and complex to be resolved in a vote for one candidate as against another. Apparently Lippmann ruled out the possibility that candidates might represent different ideologies, and that the voters could have a well-defined preference for one philosophy as against another. Yet the election victories of Mr. Roosevelt and, perhaps even more clearly, Mr. Truman's success in 1948, prove that the people evaluate issues and vote their convictions.

The rôle of the people, Lippmann thought, was extraneous to issues. The implications of public questions were beyond the grasp of the citizens. Their efforts to affect decisions he regarded as "meddling." He felt, moreover, that reading and attendance at lectures could contribute little toward solving the problem. For if the aim of such study was to develop the capacity to judge issues, only failure could result. The general public, "outsiders," could never acquire the knowledge of "insiders."

Democracy had set for itself a goal incapable of achievement in our society. It was common sense, therefore, to acknowledge it.[49] We needed an educational scheme that recognized a practical objective: to identify the party in a dispute that stood for adherence to fixed rules. He proposed that the public be trained only to distinguish the faction which by its behavior merited support.[50]

Repeatedly Lippmann has deprecated majority rule. He has maintained that when a minority acquiesces in a majority decision it bows to the force of numbers and not to "ethical superiority." Seeking to avoid civil strife, the minority simply acknowledges that it is faced with a preponderance of physical strength and surrenders without a fight. He scorned the notion that either wisdom or virtue resided in majorities,[51] and cited as proof the existence of civil-rights codes to protect minorities.[52] To "limit the power of majorities," he thought, might be a principal duty of those who loved liberty.[53]

Lippmann showed deep concern at the power of pressure

groups and expressed the belief that majorities were created by special interests with well-defined objectives. He
even went so far as to say that the "prevailing opinion is
not the opinion which the majority would hold if it understood the question and had made its decision." [54] Thereby
he implied that the majority was necessarily wrong. He
spoke disparagingly of "temporary majorities," and his references to "51 per cent" of the voters suggested that majorities were regularly achieved only by the slimmest of
margins.[55] The Federal system of checks and balances was
much to his liking; a society in which "transient" majorities could do what they wanted when they wanted to,
seemed to Lippmann "not democracy but dictatorship of
the majority." [56]

On one issue, however—the Supreme Court—Lippmann
stood squarely for majority rule. Five-to-four and six-to-
three decisions seemed reasonable to him. Lippmann explained that issues had to be resolved, that "some decision
is better than none, and that while men may honestly
differ, the majority must rule." [57] It should be noted, however, that he expressed this view at a time when the Supreme Court decisions were running heavily against the
New Deal.

The conclusion is inescapable that Lippmann pro-
foundly distrusts the concept of majority rule, and believes
that the minority must somehow be right. In one of his
clearest statements on the subject he advocated putting the
public "in its place, so that it may exercise its own powers,
but no less and perhaps even more, so that each of us may
live free of the trampling and the roar of a bewildered
herd." [58]

In his *Preface to Morals,* published in 1929, Lippmann
addressed himself to that group who rejected supernatural
faith. As a suitable "religion of the spirit" he offered what
he called "humanism." He had no quarrel with those whose
spiritual needs were being filled by conventional religion.
But he did profess to have the answer for the disenchanted,
for those who could not accept the "grandiose fiction" of

a supernatural kingdom, but who felt nevertheless that there was "no freedom in mere freedom." [59]

The "acids of modernity," he claimed, had eaten away our trust in an Omnipotence. The structure of industrial society was such that innocent reliance on the superhuman was no longer possible for large numbers of people. Yet belief of some sort was necessary. For orthodoxy gave to man a sense of organization and dignity; these derived from his identification with a larger whole. Something positive had to replace the old faith if man was not to be left spiritually adrift.

The new religion, according to Lippmann, had to lie within human experience. It had to be logical, intelligible, and relevant in a swift-changing society; essentially it had to be pragmatic. Humanism was his answer. "When men can no longer be theists, they must, if they are civilized, become humanists." [60] Unlike theistic morality, humanism could not invoke higher laws or divine sanction. While the preachers in a theistic order were above refutation, the humanist teachers had to justify themselves "by the test of mundane experience."

In contrasting humanism with theism, Lippmann maintained that the marks of theism were "dependence, obedience, [and] conformity in the presence of a superhuman power which administers reality...." [61] Humanism, on the other hand, was characterized by "detachment, understanding, and disinterestedness in the presence of reality itself." He explained "detachment" and "disinterestedness" as a kind of intellectualization of one's emotions. Instead, for example, of accepting evil as part of a divine, unalterable plan, the humanist would deal with it analytically. He would determine its character, its probable duration, and its treatment. To detach one's self from his fears and study them at a distance was to render them harmless. Instead of being possessed by them he could relegate them to a proper place in his life. [62] Lippmann pointed out the similarity of this approach to Freud's psychoanalytical "catharsis of emotion."

Humanism, Lippmann held, was the mature man's approach to belief. It promised freedom from enervating worry. It was essentially hygienic in that it brought to light deep-rooted conflicts. It enabled man to "take the world as it comes, and within himself remain quite unperturbed." Humanism assured, moreover, that happiness was not deferred to a remote future but was to be experienced here and now, for the Kingdom of God, Lippmann maintained, was within each man's bosom.[63]

Following the publication of *Preface to Morals* Lippmann's writing began increasingly to appeal to the spiritual-minded. While in *Preface to Morals* he had advocated humanism, his later work, with few exceptions, approached a spirit of theism. Materialism and "personal religion" gave way to open acknowledgment of eternal truths and Christian ethics. He inveighed against mere acquisitiveness as a goal for society; he warned government leaders that they must live on a moral plane compatible with their high official status.[64] To a group of young scholars leaving Columbia University he advocated the contemplative life, remote from the strife and tensions of a quarreling world.[65]

In *Good Society* he condemned collectivist systems on the count, among others, that they did violence to human personality. He maintained that the Russian, German, and Italian dictatorships, after they had disposed of political dissidents, "went on to attack the churches and the religious life." The authoritarians aimed to eliminate the source from which people drew strength. The "religious experience" would always inspire men to resist the dictator's pretensions. In this experience the dignity and integrity of human personality were constantly being reaffirmed. Hence religion was obnoxious to the totalitarian leaders. Collectivism was doomed; among the important reasons was its failure to recognize the sanctity of persons. No temporary success of a collectivist order could obscure this basic, unalterable fact.[66]

Lippmann's developing theism did not go unnoticed. In an article published in the Catholic weekly, *Commonweal*,

L. J. A. Mercier observed with approval Lippmann's concern for the "inviolability of man" and declared that the columnist's position was virtually in accord with that of the Catholic Church.[67]

In a Phi Beta Kappa address delivered at the University of Pennsylvania on December 29, 1940,[68] Lippmann assailed the existing educational system for its supposed neglect of the religious tradition of the west. Our culture, he pointed out, had originated in Greece. It was inherited by the Romans, and developed by the Fathers of the Church. Additions were made by countless artists, writers, scientists, and philosophers. The men who founded our country had studied this tradition. But modern education had rejected this religious and classical heritage as "no longer necessary."

In *Good Society* Lippmann had held that most men, when they reached a "middle-class standard of life," ceased to desire additional wealth; they did not consider the further aggrandizement of riches as worth the trouble, but preferred leisure and security instead. The "acquisitive psychology of the nineteenth century economic man" he found no longer operative.[69] But in a 1942 address to the American Catholic Philosophical Association he said that a chief difficulty plaguing modern man was his insatiable appetite for worldly goods.[70] Man's wants had grown to such proportions that they could never be satisfied. Lippmann deplored this irrational yearning for material things, this compulsive tendency toward "interminable acquisition." Indeed, he argued, more people were now engaged in the mad hunt for riches than before. He lamented man's incapacity to find "security and serenity in the universe," suggesting that his restless search for wealth and power was at fault. He said, moreover, that "while we talk of a standard of life, in fact we have no standard of life except that each man shall desire more than he has thus far obtained." [71]

One of the grave responsibilities facing the modern world, said Lippmann, was to deal with man's unrestrained expectations. This was, he thought, a more serious problem than giving man an adequate livelihood. His speech was innocent of any suggestion that hunger was a real concern to a sizable portion of the world's population, and that a great part of man's energy was spent in trying to satisfy elementary needs.

Lippmann advocated an ideal that he claimed arose from the classical tradition—the good life. This might be achieved by the cultivation of the "Golden Mean." Men's desires, ambitions, and appetites should be tempered by reality and made moderate. Above all, reason must be exalted. To follow the dictates of reason was to walk in God's path.[72]

In a conversation with the author in 1946, Lippmann indicated that while he adheres in general to the humanist position developed in *Preface to Morals,* he recognizes that "right and wrong are not transitory" but are, rather, "inherent in the nature of things." His utterances of late unequivocally take account of a supernatural force. The idea has taken root that he has abandoned the humanist position because it does not fill an elementary urge to "belong," but leaves the individual isolated and insecure.

Having departed at an early age from the Jewish faith into which he was born, and having grown dissatisfied with intellectual humanism, Lippmann, according to some friends, is standing now at the threshold of the Catholic Church. Nevertheless, he categorically denied to the author Walter Winchell's radio assertion that Lippmann was planning to become a Catholic.

In his earlier years Lippmann appealed strongly to the liberals and social reformers. But almost from the beginning there was an obvious and consistent good will toward "industrial statesmen." While he continued to support the liberal position in intellectual and philosophical terms, his opposition to individual New Deal measures attracted strong support among conservatives.

In deriding the concept of majority rule and the capacity of the people to understand basic issues, Lippmann identified himself with those who distrust democratic processes and favor a ruling elite.

On the question of religious belief Lippmann has clearly shifted his position. After making out a strong case for non-spiritual humanism, he has come, in recent years, to an unmistakable recognition of a supernatural infinity.

CHAPTER EIGHT

LIPPMANN: A CONTROVERSIAL FIGURE

A ROUND WALTER LIPPMANN A MILD STORM HAS BLOWN
for many years. As author, editor, lecturer, and columnist he has, of course, been much in the public
view. Having written a great deal on controversial subjects,
he has, understandably, attracted support and provoked
opposition.

Among his champions was editor William Allen White,
who in a review of Lippmann's *Interpretations 1931-1932*,[1]
found the columnist's appeal neither to the "moronic un-
derworld" nor to the "smart and sophisticated," but rather
to the nation's leaders in politics, business, and opinion-
molding. In White's view Lippmann wrote for the policy
makers of the country.[2] Earlier, White had hailed Lippmann's advent to the columns of the *Herald Tribune* as
an event of singular importance:

"Walter Lippmann's bugle call crashing through the columns of the most important Republican right wing newspaper
in America will rally forward-walking men all over America.
Moreover, it will let the conservatives know what the other
half thinks. A clearer understanding of the aims of the em-
battled but baffled liberals in a vastly complicated and uncer-
tain world will not be had elsewhere in the English language."[3]

After Lippmann had been a columnist for about a year,
Professor Allan Nevins pointed out that his articles were
essentially in the spirit of his old *World* editorials; that
while the tone of Lippmann's columns was somewhat sub-

dued, the writing conveyed a sense of earnestness and conviction. Above all, Nevins found, Lippmann's articles were distinguished by uncompromising honesty, and an authority that derived from many years of thoughtful study. These qualities, Nevins added, assured the columnist of the continued adherence of a large, heterogeneous readership.[4]

Writing in the *Saturday Review of Literature,* historian James Truslow Adams found Lippmann a leading intellectual force in our time, the heir of the great nineteenth-century editors, Godkin, Raymond, Dana, and Greeley. Adams congratulated the Ogden Reids, editors and owners of the *Herald Tribune,* for their splendid judgment in giving Lippmann a forum for the free expression of his views. Adams even went so far as to say that "what happens to Lippmann in the next decade may be of greater interest than what happens to any other single figure now on the American scene."[5] Such apotheosis, it must be admitted, has come to few journalists.

Not to be ignored among the influential supporters of Lippmann has been *Time* magazine, which in its own irreverent way has frequently indicated its high regard for the columnist.[6] When *Time* reviewed *Good Society,* Lippmann's portrait appeared on the magazine's cover, a signal distinction in itself. The book was given more than five columns of space.[7] This powerful journal quotes Lippmann frequently, oftentimes referring to him as "Pundit" Lippmann.

Commonweal began in 1936 to express gratification with Lippmann's writing.[8] In an article called "Walter Lippmann's Evolution," L. J. A. Mercier noted that the columnist had changed from a "modernist" and "humanist" to a theist.[9] Mercier found evidence of Lippmann's altered position in "On this Rock," the final chapter in *Good Society.* Here Lippmann had spoken of the "inviolability" of man. Mercier took this as proof of Lippmann's belief in an immortal soul which only God could judge. In a *Commonweal* article appearing early in 1940, the same

writer pointed out that Lippmann was to be numbered
among a group of columnists who were writing in a spirit
akin to Catholicism.[10]

Far less friendly have been the articles about Lippmann
in *Christian Century*. One of the most critical of these
stories followed his address to a Columbia graduating class.
Lippmann had urged that the scholar "build a wall against
chaos, and behind that wall . . . give his true allegiance, not
to the immediate world, but to the invisible empire of
reason." [11] The editor of *Christian Century* denounced
what he considered Lippmann's escapism, and endorsed
instead Chaplain Knox's exhortation, delivered at the same
time, that the young graduates throw themselves into the
fight for social reform.[12] The same publication assailed
Lippmann for his support of Alf Landon in 1936. It argued
that the columnist's reasons for favoring the Republican
candidate were "artificial, trivial rationalization . . . hardly
worthy of the Vox Pop column in a fifth-rate paper." It
accused Lippmann of wanting passivity in government at a
time when grave national problems called for vigorous
action.[13]

Christian Century also took exception to some of Lippmann's recommendations on foreign policy. It attacked him
for favoring outright annexation of Pacific island bases
after World War II. His proposal, they said, was an inde-
cent reversion to the old imperialism, and a betrayal of
promises made in the Atlantic Charter.[14]

Ernest Sutherland Bates, writing in the *Modern
Monthly*, declared that Lippmann's reputation for liberalism had been achieved through "a balanced style." Bates
found that Lippmann's language was philosophical "even
though his thoughts are not." [15] Moreover, said Bates, Lippmann was a vacillator. "Advocacy of revolution—abandonment of revolution—advocacy of reform—abandonment of
reform—acceptance of the opportunist present—elevating
talk of the daily incident." [16]

Perhaps the most comprehensive indictment ever penned

of Walter Lippmann was a series of four articles by Amos
Pinchot, appearing in the *Nation* during the summer of
1933. In his first essay, titled "The Great Elucidator," [17]
Pinchot found Lippmann an apologist for big business.
He accused Lippmann of having deliberately ignored the
revelations of such Congressional investigating bodies as
the Stanley Committee, which in 1911-12, after painstaking
research, had spelled out the unsavory facts about the steel
business. Instead, Pinchot said, Lippmann had imputed
to industry "a regenerative, self-rectifying principle that
combats greed and makes for the subordination of sordid to
enlightened aims." [18] By turning his back on the findings
that did not suit his thesis, Pinchot added, Lippmann had
betrayed the scientific method which he had always espoused.

In his second article, "The New Tammany," [19] Pinchot
maintained that Lippmann had wobbled on the Tammany
Hall issue, depending upon his prevailing interest. When,
as editor of the *World,* Lippmann had favored Al Smith
for President, he had written of a "new" Tammany. Editor
Lippmann had painted the ancient Wigwam in appealing
tones and pronounced Smith's affiliation natural and innocent. But in 1932, said Pinchot, when Lippmann was
writing against the candidacy of Governor Franklin D.
Roosevelt, the columnist had pointed repeatedly to Roosevelt's Tammany associations in an effort to injure his
status as a candidate.

In "Obfuscator de Luxe" [20] Pinchot conceded that Lippmann's writing was marked by sparkle, polish, and per-
suasiveness. But, asked Pinchot, was it clear? He had his
doubts. Lippmann's frequent citation of foreign, unfamil-
iar sources afforded but slight illumination. Pinchot objected, moreover, to Lippmann's admiration for Alexander
Hamilton, "the first strong advocate of plutocratic fascism
in America." Beyond all else, Pinchot argued, Lippmann
had constituted himself a good-will ambassador to the rich
businessmen, seeking to convert them to the rôle of industrial statesmen, disinterested and conscious of the public

welfare. Far from achieving his objective, Pinchot remarked, Lippmann himself had been taken in completely
by men of wealth; he was, in effect, voicing their views.[21]

The final article in the series [22] was an effort to prove
that Lippmann was an enemy of democracy. Pinchot argued that *Public Opinion*, and especially *Phantom Public*
added up to a refutation of the democratic way of life, and
advocated, by indirection, some kind of fascist regime. The
two books, said Pinchot, gave "innumerable and apparently
insurmountable objections to democracy." [23] In Pinchot's
view the failures of our form of government were caused
not by any inherent defects but because of the machina-
tions of a powerful, privilege-hunting minority, the very
group Lippmann had exculpated. Pinchot concluded that
Lippmann had done his readers a vast amount of harm:
he had confused their thinking; he had soothed them to
sleep when the public welfare had called for vigilance; he
had pictured big business as a wise, unselfish leadership;
he had, like plutocracy itself, distrusted the people and
popular processes; he had diverted attention from the fight
between privilege and justice; above all, he had offered
complacency instead of truth.[24] Later, it should be added,
Pinchot's attitude toward Lippmann softened somewhat.
He gave a generally favorable review to *Good Society*.[25]

It is not surprising that the Communist organ, *New
Masses*, regarded Lippmann with disfavor. Corliss Lamont
complained that in the years since the Russian revolution
Lippmann had never taken the trouble to visit the Soviet
Union. Lamont thought this a "remarkable record" for
"one who purports to be an impartial and reliable commentator on world affairs...." [26] The same writer, review-
ing *Good Society*, found Lippmann a spokesman for big
business and the advocate of an era long since vanished.[27]
New Masses published another hostile article on September 10, 1940, Barbara Giles' "Pundit in a Penthouse." [28]
In an altogether different vein, however, was Joseph Starobin's "The Heart of Foreign Policy." [29] Starobin found, in
this deferential review of Lippmann's *U.S. Foreign Policy*,

"a fertile and extremely provocative thesis...." The reviewer liked Lippmann's plan for a "nuclear alliance" to include the United States, Great Britain, and the Soviet Union.

John T. Flynn, writing before the 1936 election, maintained that Lippmann, in coming out for Landon, had at last betrayed his real sympathies: he was a Republican. Flynn ridiculed Lippmann's reasons for supporting the Kansan and argued that Lippmann's views coincided with those of business leaders. He charged that Lippmann's hostility to NRA, the stock-exchange act, the munitions investigation, and the holding-company act proved Lippmann's adherence to the cause of big finance. "When that the poor banker and broker hath cried," said Flynn, "Lippmann hath wept." [30]

In a similar spirit Bruce Bliven of the *New Republic* rejected Lippmann's arguments on behalf of Landon. Bliven remarked, "I do not doubt the sincerity of the mental processes that have brought him to believe that Governor Landon, if elected, will do the same things as Mr. Roosevelt, only better." [31]

Heywood Broun found Lippmann too vulnerable to ignore. Lippmann had urged President Roosevelt to reexamine his "premises" and "methods." Broun scorned any such approach and argued in favor of moving vigorously in one direction without stopping too often along the way to reconsider. Broun noted that he had been watching Lippmann's bi-directional progress since their freshman days at Harvard. Lippmann, he said, was "quite apt to score a field goal for Harvard and a touchdown for Yale in one and the same play. But, of course, he specializes in safeties." Broun attested, nevertheless, to Lippmann's "sincerity and...devotion to truth and the public weal." [32]

With somewhat less amiability Broun criticized what he regarded as Lippmann's tenderness toward the utilities, and his concern for the minority in the 1936 election. Broun asked why Lippmann didn't also champion the (liberal) minority on the Supreme Court. Broun added that "minorities are often gallant and sometimes correct, but I doubt that any democracy can be built on the principle of loser take all." [33]

Max Lerner, also, took exception to what he called Lippmann's desire to "entrench minority rule." Lippmann, he said, favored an interpretation of the Constitution that would require every new piece of social legislation "to run the gauntlet of a two-thirds vote of Congress and a three-quarters vote of the states. This would be minority rule with a vengeance." [34] When he reviewed *Good Society* Lerner made it clear that Lippmann's integrity was not in question. Nor, he added, did he subscribe to the notion that Lippmann had "sold out." But Lippmann was now advocating "the liberalism of the right; the catchwords have remained the same, but the content is the opposite of what it was." Lerner concluded that "Mr. Lippmann's brand of liberalism is the intellectual garment of capitalist power...." [35]

Margaret Marshall, literary editor of the *Nation,* thought that Lippmann would have been happy in the rôle of a British earl half a century ago. She found his concern for the free market "antique" and irrelevant. His solutions to the great problems of the day she thought "impossibilist" and calculated only to confirm big business in their prevailing practices. She maintained, further, that Lippmann drew on his liberal stock-in-trade sufficiently to maintain a standing-of-sorts as a progressive. He "preaches the futility of any attempt to deal with modern problems in their own terms and thereby rationalizes and blesses the status quo. No wonder business men feel elevated and enlightened when the Great Elucidator expresses their humble opinions in the best prose on the market...." [36]

Lippmann's advocacy of a return to the classics and his impatience with instruction in vocational subjects drew the fire of various educators. President Harry D. Gideonse of Brooklyn College, while admitting that much was wrong with present-day education, scoffed at the idea that reconstructing the curriculum around the classics would provide the cure. Little help, Gideonse said, would come from "nostalgic idealization of a past that never was." [37]

As a leading interpreter of public affairs, Lippmann has built up a large body of supporters. To this group Lippmann's analyses represent indispensable, authoritative intelligence on contemporary problems. At the same time he has alienated other readers, who feel that he has lost his direction. This group, while they acknowledge his high competence, deplore what they regard as his failure to adhere steadfastly to a militantly liberal position. They have been articulate and unsparing in their criticism.

CHAPTER NINE

LIPPMANN TODAY AND TOMORROW

M UCH, UNDOUBTEDLY TOO MUCH, HAS BEEN MADE
of the fact that in the course of his career Walter
Lippmann has changed his position on certain controversial issues. His honesty and his convictions have been
brought into question by critics who have, apparently,
been unwilling to recognize that events and issues acquire
new perspectives with the passing of time; that to change
one's mind does not necessarily suggest a lack of virtue;
that sometimes the test of courage lies in the modification
of one's course rather than in adherence to it. Nor, apparently, have some of his readers made sufficient allowance
for the fact that much of his writing is done under pressure
and reflects transitory opinions that at the time of writing
appeared to him true and significant.

There is no basis for the charge that Lippmann is an
opportunist who abandoned the poor and grubby left for
the rich, plushy right. His socialist affiliation, it has been
shown, was tenuous and impermanent in character; moreover it cannot be said that he has come to rest in the conservative camp. He has, rather, remained a good deal of an
independent spirit. His pronouncements, while they undoubtedly suggest a right-of-center orientation, have many
times discomforted if not pained his well-to-do followers.
He is assuredly not the mouthpiece of plutocratic wealth
in this country. A good deal of an eclectic, he has sometimes taken "liberal," at other times "conservative" view-

points. His opponents have seen this as inconstancy at best, a lack of belief and integrity at worst. "... once a votary in the house of Marx," wrote Amos Pinchot, "our Elucidator now worships in the house of Morgan." [1] That Lippmann can be quoted on either side of certain issues is evidence less of vacillation than of judgments modified by study and experience.

In certain respects Walter Lippmann exhibits qualities that our social psychologists have identified with upper-middle-class intellectuals. His notable tendency to write "balanced" essays, in which left and right are alternately blamed and praised; his consistent efforts to smooth over conflict by urging the application of reason; his unquestioned respect for the moralities, and, in a sense, the Puritan tradition; his obvious concern for appearances; his respect for learning; above all his support for liberal theories of social reform coupled with frequent disapproval of the actual legislation, are part of an identifiable pattern—the upper-middle-class intellectual.

Lippmann's closest friends have testified to his ability —even his compulsion—to see many sides of a problem. This is true in spite of his tendency in recent years to associate with conservatives. He could not, if he wanted to, become the literary hireling of reactionary wealth, any more than he could remain a socialist. As an informed, sensitive intellectual he is necessarily aware of the human aspect of great issues. The principles he proclaims are and always have been in the humanitarian tradition. But when ordinary mortals were seeking to translate philosophy into legislative reality, Lippmann gave little help. He raised so many objections that his principles themselves became suspect.

Symbolic of Lippmann's irresolution on the "left versus right" issue is this much-told tale. A certain hostess, distinguished and wealthy, decided to play a game. She directed all her guests who believed in capitalism to line up on one side of the room; those who believed in socialism to go to the other side. The company divided, with the sole exception of Walter Lippmann, who remained in the middle of the floor.

Much of the controversy concerning Lippmann revolves around his "liberalism." This word has meant different things to him at different times. This is perhaps understandable. Disturbing to the reader of Lippmann's books and columns, however, is the suspicion that to Lippmann "liberalism" has meant different things at the same time.

From 1913, when he began his writing career, up to 1935, including the years he spent on the *New Republic* and the *World,* Lippmann may be said to have adhered rather steadfastly to a "progressive" position. He applauded the policies of Theodore Roosevelt, Woodrow Wilson, and Al Smith. He fought the Ku Klux Klan, the Sacco-Vanzetti decision, and peonage in Florida. He advocated trade unionism and the humanizing of industry. He supported social security and, for the unemployed, public works rather than handouts. During this period, as later, he was independent and not an adherent of any party or movement. But the conclusion is clear that within reasonable limits his stand on economic and social issues was the "liberal" one.

In 1934 he wrote *Method of Freedom* in which he championed the rôle of government as an instrument for preserving economic equilibrium in the nation. The total resources of government, he emphasized, should be kept available to correct any imbalance in the economy. This thesis he confirmed a year later in the *New Imperative.*

His columns on the New Deal were generally favorable until 1935. Before Mr. Roosevelt's first inauguration the columnist pleaded that the new President be invested with full power to carry through a comprehensive program of reform. But even while Lippmann supported the New Deal in principle, he took exception to the specific measures that gave body to the New Deal philosophy. He had emphasized repeatedly in his columns, books, and speeches that the unemployed should be given jobs on public works; he had applauded Mr. Roosevelt's conviction along the same lines. Nevertheless Lippmann thought the President's public-works program demoralizing, while Mr. Roosevelt's approach was that of a "Tory philanthropist."

Lippmann had proscribed the dole but in the face of a mounting deficit his objections grew faint. He had argued the need of legislation to regulate the utilities and had even endorsed the Holding-Company Bill. But when the Administration fought for a system of adequate control, Lippmann's support was on the other side. Though Lippmann had told with eloquence the dangers inherent in a society of plutocrats and paupers, he denounced the so-called "soak-the-rich" tax plan. Yet this measure seemed to be a reasonable implementation of a principle Lippmann had espoused.

Despite the stirring pieces he had written on behalf of social security he found little that was acceptable in the measure as finally drawn. He even denounced it at one point as "a pipe...laid into the treasury...." He opposed the first AAA and the Wagner Act, the latter called by labor its Magna Carta. In 1932, when he wanted the Democrats to win he warned that a Hoover victory would mean a hopeless schism between Republican Executive and Democratic Congress. In 1936, when he sought a Landon victory he said that to have a Republican President and a Democratic legislature would mean a "national," bipartisan government in which co-operation would be a certainty.

Lippmann came to believe that the New Deal was something more than the "free collectivism" he had advocated in *Method of Freedom*. He seems to have concluded, rather, that the New Dealers were socialists trying to refashion our economy along collectivist lines.[2] Beginning in 1935 he expressed his suspicion that Mr. Roosevelt had such a scheme in mind. In the months before the 1936 election the columnist repeated the charge many times. He argued that the growing "centralization" imperilled the national defense, that Mr. Roosevelt's re-election would be bad for the President, the Democratic Party, and the country. His pre-election articles were innocent of any suggestion that another victory for Mr. Roosevelt might constitute a valid demonstration that the people approved his course and favored a continuation of his policies.

In *Good Society* Lippmann re-examined the meaning of "liberalism." He concluded that all "collectivist" states, whether totalitarian or "gradualist," represented a negation of liberalism. Adam Smith, he thought, had been the true philosopher and prophet of the liberal movement. Lippmann argued that the industrial revolution had made necessary a market economy where goods and services could be freely exchanged. Such an economy meant both prosperity and liberty. Planning, he said, disrupted the freedom of the market and was therefore to be avoided. Furthermore, to plan successfully required an order of genius that the race had not yet produced.

Up to this point Lippmann's argument suggested that he was favoring a return to laissez faire. But this was far from the case. He categorically rejected laissez faire, calling it a "disease" that had affected the old liberalism. There was, he said, a valid body of reforms, an "Agenda of Liberalism" that the market economy made necessary. The state had to insure the honesty of weights and measures; it had to protect the consumer in his purchases and the laborer facing a powerful employer. The state had to make certain that the markets were efficient and honest. It had, moreover, to conserve and improve the nation's resources, both human and physical. This meant large expenditures on eugenics, education, recreation, and public works. He emphasized that the true liberalism did not tolerate waste, exploitation, or aggrandizement by the powerful at the expense of the weak. He condemned holding companies and monopolies as artificial structures that violated the principles of a free-working market.

The necessary regulatory functions of the liberal state were to be carried out by a staff who recognized that their official function conveyed no special privileges; that they were at all times agents of the state and never superior to the citizens. Above all, Lippmann urged, they should be of a "judicial" temperament.

The question that projects itself after reading Lippmann's "Agenda of Liberalism" is whether the reforms he feels are necessary could possibly be effected without that very "planning" and "bureaucracy" he is at such pains to discredit; whether, in other words, he can have his reforms without reformers, his bureaus without bureaucrats. There is no reason to believe he can.

Monopoly, said Lippmann, restricted production. To that degree it was injurious to the market economy. Every monopoly, he added, functioned by virtue of some kind of legal privilege. Therefore, he said, the way to end monopoly was to change the law. It is difficult to believe that Lippmann could seriously offer such a solution to this problem. The history of governmental efforts to control monopoly stands as refutation to Lippmann's idea.[3]

No less strange was his proposal of "legal remedies" as a substitute for regulation by government.[4] Regulatory bureaus and agencies would, under his scheme, be very greatly reduced. Individuals who believed themselves wronged would have recourse to courts of law. Such a plan, it would seem, would on the one hand be a hardship to the individual of small means who sustained injuries at the hands of a powerful adversary; on the other hand, if the innumerable adjustments achieved by government agencies had to be decided by regular tribunals, there would have to be a fantastic proliferation of the nation's courts. His proposal raises the spectre of litigation on a scale hitherto unknown. There is the gravest doubt that his plan would be an improvement on the evil of government bureaucracy.

The reader of Lippmann's books and columns does not get a clear picture of what he stands for in regard to government intervention in social and economic areas. The emerging pattern is confusing. From a long devotion to the "liberal" cause, including strong endorsement of the New Deal philosophy, Lippmann grew steadily more hos-

tile to the Roosevelt program. He found fault with one
New Deal measure after another, though he had previously
endorsed almost each one in principle. Then, in his book,
Good Society, he wrote at length against "collectivism,"
and made it clear that he regarded the New Deal as one
of the several species of "collectivism." But he included in
Good Society a program of social reform that strongly re-
sembles the very New Deal he had so often assailed. Moreover, in his recent book, *U.S. War Aims,* he emphatically
reaffirmed the government's economic and social responsibilities. This scheme is difficult to follow and seems to
consist of proposals that cancel each other out: the free
market combined with a broad program of social legislation. Lippmann's record suggests that his enthusiasm for
reform measures ends at the point where they are written
into law. For while he has steadily professed liberal principles, he has often recoiled from liberal enactments. There
is even some reason to suspect that Lippmann's "liberalism" is a philosophic concept incapable of translation into
reality.

In extenuation it might be said that Mr. Lippmann's
failure to support liberal legislation as ardently as he has
supported liberal principles might be a result of his unusual ability to see inferences. Repeatedly he charged that
New Deal measures were being framed by ignorant enthu-
siasts who, though they intended well, were acting hastily
and without a proper regard for the history of welfare
legislation. It is probably true that only a few of the New
Deal leaders had Lippmann's background in political science, philosophy, and economics. He foresaw difficulties
that possibly never occurred to the men around the President. Because he believed that many New Deal enactments
were defective, he rejected them. But his efforts, obviously,
served the cause of the President's opponents.

Lippmann's counsels of perfection seemed to the New
Dealers well calculated to obstruct the whole reform pro-
gram. He feared, for example, that elections under the
Wagner Act might show a "plurality" rather than a "ma-

jority"; that the insurance fund of the Social Security Act would quickly be exhausted and payments would then become a mere government dole; that wages-and-hours legislation, instead of improving the status of the low-paid Southern worker, would damage Southern industry by depriving it of its "natural" advantages; that the Murray Full Employment Bill had erred in designating gainful employment a "right." It would be better to call full employment a government "policy" instead. Lippmann, it must be remembered, had in *Method of Freedom* insisted on the *right* to work as a basic liberty of modern man.

Defending Lippmann's unfriendly treatment of the New Deal, some writers insist that it is the columnist's function to criticize and point out shortcomings, rather than to praise. They hold, further, that a "lack of dissent" on the part of the column writer implies assent. But this argument ignores the basic fact that the credulous reader is likely to accept the word of his favorite commentator; that when a columnist disapproves a measure he is assumed to mean it. Few readers, moreover, are equipped to perform the subtle task of deciding where a "lack of dissent" implies assent.

The columnist, perhaps even more than the writer of books, must have a great facility with words. Especially is this true of a commentator who writes on major problems of the day. The deadline, bane of newspaperdom, is an ever-present reality to him. In spite of this handicap to serious newspaper comment, Lippmann's columns have achieved a high degree of literary excellence. As a technician with words, he has shown consistently high skill. Nor has he been content, with rare exceptions, to camouflage a paucity of ideas with verbiage. His columns have not suffered from a lack of meaningful content. In virtually all his expositions there is to be found a solid core of informed thought. He has done relatively little "thumb-sucking," the fairly common practice of newspapermen to expound self-generated theories and syllogisms. To his credit is the fact that he reads extensively, and consults very frequently with key persons in national and international affairs. The available evidence shows, regrettably, that his friendships and associations are almost exclusively with the more important figures in politics, diplomacy, business, and the arts; that he is isolated from labor and farm people, and the leaders of minority groups. This suggests an aversion, conscious or unconscious, to the great mass movements that are a significant—if inelegant—part of the present-day world.

His writing, intended for an audience of superior intelligence, reads smoothly. It is clear, logical, and inevitably persuasive. It is free of exhortation and seldom shows anger or alarm. Its power derives from a sense of objectivity and implied authority. Above all it appears to be disinterested and reasonable, the product of a sober, responsible thinker.

Only infrequently does Lippmann stumble into generalizations. He hedges carefully, and has had, therefore, to recant relatively few of his statements. His influence has been on the side of temperate judgment and restraint in evaluating issues and men.

The mature Lippmann only slightly suggests the young Lippmann who could write, in approval of the English suffragettes, that "unfortunately, in this world great issues are not won by good manners." As he grew older he became increasingly concerned about the niceties in human relationships, and sought to lift issues from the level of combat to the plane of reason and good will. On some matters this approach has made sense; on others it has been the ultimate in unreality. It has even appeared, occasionally, that he has been more eager for seemly behavior than for the maintenance of basic principles. A case in point was his rejection of the proposal by the Commission on Freedom of the Press that the press engage in vigorous mutual criticism. This is perhaps an outstanding instance of his distaste for controversy, even when an important social purpose was at stake. Members of the press, it would seem, are supremely well qualified to expose deception and dishonesty on the part of newspapers. But Lippmann would have none of this kind of thing.

Yet he knew the shortcomings of the American press as well as any of his professional brothers. As long ago as 1920, in a brilliant study called "A Test of the News," he went on record as favoring higher standards in journalism: improved reporting, an end to the editorializing of news, and the creation of militant outside agencies that would effectively supervise the press.[5] The same year he published *Liberty and the News*,[6] in which he argued that newspapers, as "common carriers" ought properly to be brought under "social control" as a necessary means of safeguarding the readers. He deplored the power wielded by publishers and demanded the "fearless and relentless exposure" of newspaper falsehoods. He insisted on the need for a press accountable to the public. The Commission on Freedom of the Press, in its recent report echoed many of the principles enunciated by Lippmann over a quarter-century ago.

It may be said categorically that in his rigid personal adherence to the principles of ethical journalism Lippmann's record is extraordinarily good. The only criticism to which he might properly be subject stems from his unreadiness to battle for the general improvement of newspaper standards. Once an ardent protagonist, he is, apparently, no longer actively concerned with the reform of the press.

Occasionally Lippmann's words have suggested a detachment from reality. This is true of a speech he gave in 1942, "Man's Image of Man,"[7] in which he put forth the view that the "characteristic misery of our age" was man's "unlimited and therefore insatiable desire" for worldly goods. There was no hint in his statement that privation was a genuine problem anywhere in the world. The basic difficulty, said Lippmann, was not in "providing an adequate material existence" but in meeting man's boundless expectations. He clearly implied that if man would only adjust his wants "to the reality of things" he would begin to experience the good life. For a man in Lippmann's

economic station to expound such a view was either supreme naïveté or a mighty indifference to the problem of
survival faced by most of the world.

Although Lippmann has clarified countless individual
issues for his readers, he has offered a number of interpretations of dubious merit. His denial that businessmen
were primarily motivated by the search for profit has certainly not been sustained by events. His statement that
large-scale business, by virtue of its size, became "public"
in character was no contribution to the solution of a complex problem. It could only disarm his readers and blur
their understanding of the need for regulatory legislation.
His denunciation of the Wagner Labor Relations Act as
"reactionary" surely represented a tortured construction of
that measure. His failure adequately to appraise fascism,
and his belief that fascism was "un-American ... un-Belgian, un-German and un-English" because it was "un-industrial" suggest a serious blind spot in this long-time student of economics.

In *Good Society* Lippmann asserted that the New Deal
was "collectivist" and that "collectivism" meant poverty
and governmental tyranny. He also lumped together the
New Deal and totalitarian communism and fascism. This
was extravagant and ill-considered even if innocent. Moreover, he occasionally refuted his own charge by finding, in
his columns, that the New Deal was in the American tradition.

Repeatedly Lippmann deplored what he considered the
neglect of the classics in modern education. Present-day
political leaders, he thought, lacked the insight that a
study of the great works of the past would have given
them; hence they were particularist and sectional in their
outlook. But the Founding Fathers, he said, having had in
common a classical training, knew the great questions of
their time and were able to take the large view. Lippmann
seemed to have forgotten that the Constitutional Convention was riven by sectional and state-rights feeling.

Modern education, according to Lippmann, consisted

basically in preparing youth for specific livelihoods. Its success, he thought, was measured by this yardstick. The great, abiding truths that the race had produced had been cast aside in favor of a shallow, specific body of data that bore little relation to man's cultural history. The growth of reason, which followed inevitably from the old, classical education was now neglected. Education had been "emptied of its content"; our youth knew of the classics by hearsay alone. Modern educators, he held, fearful of the discipline that the old learning required, had converted the school from a house of learning to "a mere training ground for personal careers."

Lippmann's concept is an exclusive one. Put into general practice it would mean the education of that minority who are capable of assimilating the classical tradition. He did not suggest what should be done with the others.

Frequently Lippmann has betrayed his impatience, even his contempt, for the idea of majority rule. In *Public Opinion* he asked for "intelligence bureaus" to sift data and interpret them for a people unable to do it for themselves. In *Phantom Public* he went further, denying that the people could utilize the findings of the "experts." The most that could be expected of them, he said, was to decide which of the actors in a dispute were behaving according to settled rules. It was, he felt, beyond the capacity of our citizens to keep informed on the numberless issues clamoring for attention. The facts were too numerous, too complicated, and often too obscure for ordinary people to understand; nor was it reasonable to expect the citizens to spend time and energy to acquire the intelligence necessary to render informed judgments. Such tasks, he maintained, were beyond the people's ability; the myth of the "omnicompetent citizen" should be exposed. The individuals directly concerned with issues should decide them. They should be freed, he said, from the interference of "ignorant and meddlesome outsiders."

After granting that these views were honestly reached and cogently stated, it must still be added that they stemmed from a kind of defeatism. If Lippmann's thesis is valid the prevailing ideal of democracy must be sharply narrowed. Instead of working toward broad participation in public affairs we should support the notion of an intellectual and administrative elite. Since he elaborated these views Lippmann's references to public opinion have been free of a positive plan for developing the people's ability to judge major issues in our society as it is presently constructed. What is more serious, however, is the strong implication that he does not believe such a program is even possible.

Experts in civic instruction have long admitted the hardships besetting their efforts to build competence in this field. Inertia, ignorance, and the corrupting efforts of self-seekers magnify the difficulties. But progress has been made. The political intelligence of the American people is, unquestionably, greater than ever before. With improved schools and better instruction there is reason to believe that advances in this direction will continue. This is not to suggest that all our people can or should be expected to acquire understanding of the great problems before them. But because perfection will never be achieved is a poor reason to abandon the objective.

To his writing Walter Lippmann has brought a rich and informed background of continuing scholarship in economics, history, government, and philosophy. With great intelligence and earnestness he has sought to interpret for his readers day-to-day problems and long-range issues. In considerable measure he has succeeded in his endeavors. But despite his best efforts he has judged events according to his own particular body of stereotypes. And there is little reason to believe that Walter Lippmann's stereotypes represent the realities of history more truly than those of any other person of superior native endowment and training in public affairs.

He has not been an impartial witness. His judgments, however pure their purpose, have reinforced existing social and economic relationships and have militated against redressing glaring inequities.

He has not been the people's columnist. In the words of one shrewd observer, "One could forgive Walter Lippmann many things if his heart really bled for humanity." And this explains why he has not achieved the greatness his youth promised. For greatness seldom comes to the overly cautious, the calmly analytical, and the supremely judicious. William Allen White's buoyant hope that Lippmann's "bugle call" would "rally forward-walking men all over America" has not been realized; nor has White's expectation that Lippmann would "let the conservatives know what the other half thinks." On the contrary, Lippmann has more often let the liberals know what the conservatives think.

There is no basis for regarding Mr. Lippmann as a "seer." Such a rôle is, of course, furthest from his own conception of his position. Any tendency to rely on him as a source of final authority is unwarranted. He is to be read with skepticism, with the feeling that his views are the serious reflections of a highly literate, well-informed mind, but also with the feeling that he has been wrong before and will very likely err again.

Walter Lippmann has dignified his calling by the tirelessness of his labors, by the high literary quality of his writing, and the industry with which he has pursued facts. He has come close to being the scholar in journalism. His views, nevertheless, are to be taken as suggestive rather than definitive.

The public interest makes it imperative that the other columnists, most of whom have neither the talent nor training of Walter Lippmann, be even more subject to careful scrutiny.

NOTES

CHAPTER ONE

1. *Herald Tribune,* Sept. 8, 1931.

2. *Public Speaking Memorabilia, Ninth Inter-class Debate,* 1905 vs. 1906. Book in possession of Franklin School (successors to the Sachs School), 18 West 89th Street.

3. *Public Speaking Memorabilia,* Tenth Inter-Class Debate, 1906 vs. 1907.

4. *Public Speaking Memorabilia.*

5. Granville Hicks, *John Reed* (New York, Macmillan, 1936), p. 34.

6. They were divorced in 1937. The following year Walter Lippmann married Helen Byrne Armstrong, formerly the wife of Hamilton Fish Armstrong.

7. "Walter Lippman: The Career of Comrade Fool," *Modern Monthly,* Vol. VII (Jun. 1933), pp. 266-274.

8. "An Open Mind: William James," *Everybody's,* Vol. XXIII (Dec. 1910), pp. 800-801.

9. *Preface to Politics* (New York, Macmillan, 1913), pp. 182-183.

10. *Ibid.,* p. 183.

11. *Ibid.,* p. x.

12. Pp. 286-289, 302-304, 315-317.

13. (New York, Kennerley), pp. 309-313.

14. (Little, Brown, Boston), 402 pp.

15. "Walter Lippmann," an autobiographical statement; *Harvard College Class of 1910.* p. 446.

16. Quoted in *The New York Times,* Oct. 13, 1946, p. 17.

17. Lippmann, "Notes for a Biography," *New Republic,* Vol. LXIII (Jul. 16, 1930), p. 251.

18. An account of The Inquiry's work may be found in Shotwell's *At the Paris Peace Conference* (New York, Macmillan, 1937), pp. 3-19.

19. Shotwell, *op. cit.*, p. 6.

20. Conversation with Mr. Lippmann, Oct. 31, 1946. Cf. Charles Seymour, Ed., *The Intimate Papers of Colonel House* (Boston, Houghton Mifflin, 1938), Vol. III, pp. 319-322.

21. Quoted in Heber Blankenhorn, *Adventures in Propaganda* (Boston, Houghton Mifflin, 1919), Appendix II, p. 161.

22. Conversation with Mr. Lippmann, Oct. 31, 1946. Cf. Seymour, *op. cit.*, Vol. IV, pp. 152-158.

23. "Walter Lippmann," *United Nations World*, Vol. I (May, 1947), p. 80.

24. "Today and Tomorrow," Apr. 1, 1937.

25. Herbert Bayard Swope, in a letter published in the *American Mercury*, Vol. LX (May, 1945), p. 632. Mr. Swope commented that "Lippmann gave magnificent support to certain new crusades in which the *World* was engaged, although he had little to do with originating them."

26. "The End of Convict Leasing in Alabama," *Literary Digest*, Vol. XCVIII (Jul. 21, 1928), p. 11.

27. Memorandum to writer, Jan. 16, 1948.

28. "It Seems to Heywood Broun," *Nation*, Vol. CXXV (Sept. 14, 1927), p. 243. Other members of Dr. Lowell's committee were Dr. Samuel W. Stratton, President of Massachusetts Institute of Technology, and Robert Grant, a writer and former judge.

29. "It Seems to Heywood Broun," *Nation*, Vol. CXXVI (May 4, 1928), p. 532.

30. "The End of the 'World' " *New Freeman*, Vol. II (Mar. 11, 1931), pp. 610-612.

31. Letter to author from Mr. Cain, Oct. 1, 1947.

32. "Walter Lippmann," New York *Herald Tribune*, Sept. 11, 1932.

33. Memorandum from Allan Nevins, Jan. 16, 1948.

CHAPTER TWO

1. In this chapter appear many terms describing Lippmann's prose. In an effort to give these passages objective validity the author compared fifteen columns by Lippmann with an equal number by his distinguished colleague of *The New York Times,* Anne O'Hare McCormick. The comparison seemed to give strong justification for the selection of terms used to describe Lippmann. Columns appearing in the Fall of 1947, dealing with the Marshall Plan, were the basis for the analysis.

2. "Washington Background," *House and Garden*, Vol. LXXXV (Jun., 1944), pp. 42-43.

3. "Walter Lippmann," New York *Herald Tribune*, Sept. 11, 1932.

4. T. and T., Jun. 14, 1934.
5. Pp. 77-100.
6. T. and T., Mar. 12, 1933.
7. (Boston, Little, Brown, 1944), pp. 173-174.
8. Letter to the author from Mr. Cain, Oct. 1, 1947.
9. *Public Opinion* (New York, Macmillan, 1922), p. 151.
10. *Ibid.*, p. 159.
11. *Ibid.*, p. 154.
12. *Ibid.*, pp. 92-93.
13. T. and T., Dec. 7, 1933.
14. T. and T., Oct. 10, 1933.
15. "Scholar in a Troubled World," *Atlantic Monthly*, Vol. CL (Aug. 1932), p. 151.
16. *Ibid.*
17. P. x.
18. T. and T., Sept. 22, 1936.
19. T. and T., Nov. 14, 1936.
20. *Time*, Vol. LII (Oct. 4, 1948), p. 52.
21. Reprinted from the *Baltimore Sun* of Apr. 10, 1935 in the New York *Herald Tribune*, Apr. 11, 1935.
22. New York *Herald Tribune*, Apr. 13, 1935.
23. *A Free and Responsible Press* (Chicago, University of Chicago Press, 1947), p. 94.
24. *Time*, Vol. XLIX (Apr. 7, 1947), p. 27.
25. "Scholar in a Troubled World," p. 152.
26. The author tested samples of columns over a five year period. The formula is given in Rudolf Flesch, *The Art of Plain Talk* (New York, Harper and Brothers, 1946), 210 pp.
27. Information on the subscriber-papers was supplied by the Herald Tribune Syndicate. Circulation figures were taken from *Editor and Publisher* 1947 International Year Book Number, Vol. LXXX (Jan. 31, 1947), 352 pp. Figures on the Latin American circulation, totaling 710,000, were supplied by Editors Press Service, New York City, in charge of syndication to Latin America.
28. *Fortune*, Vol. XXI (Jan. 1940), pp. 90-92. The *Fortune* Survey is conducted by the firm of Elmo Roper.
29. Bureau of Applied Social Research, Columbia University, "To What Extent Are Newspaper Columnists Read?" (March, 1947), p. 21.
30. *Fortune*, p. 92. In general, more Republicans than Democrats read columns.
31. (Advertising Research Foundation, New York, 1946), 64 pp.
32. Vol. XXX (Sept. 27, 1937), p. 47.

CHAPTER THREE

1. T. and T., Jun. 13, 1934.

2. Many of Lippmann's friends from the Harvard and *New Republic* days make this accusation. It is discussed by Ernest Sutherland Bates, "The Career of Comrade Fool," *loc. cit.* See also John T. Flynn, "Other People's Money," *New Republic,* Vol. LXXXVIII (Sept. 23, 1936), pp. 183-184.

3. *Preface to Politics,* pp. 287-289.

4. *Drift and Mastery,* pp. 32-33.

5. "Life is Cheap," Vol. I (Dec. 19, 1914), pp. 12-14; also "The Campaign Against Sweating," Vol. II (Mar. 27, 1915), pp. 1-8.

6. T. and T., Jun. 22, 1933.

7. T. and T., Feb. 1, 1934.

8. T. and T., Feb. 1; Apr. 20; Apr. 26, 1934.

9. T. and T., May 30, 1934.

10. (New York, Macmillan, 1934), 117 pp.

11. *Method of Freedom,* p. 36.

12. *Ibid.,* p. 46.

13. *Ibid.,* p. 57.

14. *Ibid.,* p. 56.

15. *Ibid.,* pp. 96-98.

16. *Ibid.,* p. 104.

17. *Ibid.,* p. 109.

18. *Ibid.,* p. 107. When the Murray Full Employment Bill of 1945 made "remunerative, regular and full-time employment" a "right" Lippmann objected. See "Lippmann and the Social Security Program," Chap. V.

19. *Method of Freedom,* p. 109.

20. *Ibid.,* pp. 111-112.

21. T. and T., Jan. 8, 1935.

22. (New York, Macmillan, 1935), 52 pp.

23. *New Imperative* (New York, Macmillan, 1935), p. 1.

24. T. and T., Aug. 20, 1935. See also T. and T., May 4; Jun. 8, 1935; and Lippmann's "Deepest Issue of Our Time," *Vital Speeches,* Vol. II (Jul. 1, 1936), pp. 602-604.

25. (Boston, Little, Brown), 402 pp.

26. Cf. Lippmann's *U. S. War Aims* (Boston, Little, Brown, 1944), p. 87, n. For a brief statement of the views expressed in *Good Society* see his "Providential State," *Atlantic,* Vol. CLVIII (Oct., 1936), pp. 403-412.

27. *Good Society,* p. 175.

28. *Ibid.,* pp. 48-53.

29. *Ibid.,* p. 204.

30. *Ibid.,* p. 330. See also "Providential State," *loc. cit.,* p. 403.

31. *Good Society,* p. 204.
32. *Ibid.,* pp. 16-19.
33. *Ibid.,* p. 180.
34. *Ibid.,* p. 177.
35. *Ibid.,* p. 181.
36. *Ibid.,* p. 205, n.
37. *Ibid.,* pp. 192-193.
38. *Ibid.,* pp. 108-110.
39. *Ibid.,* p. 367.
40. T. and T., May 12, 1936. See also *Good Society,* p. 106, and T. and T., May 3, 1938, in which Lippmann referred to "the whole of NRA and AAA and much of the relief and public-works policy of this Administration" as "collectivist."
41. *Good Society,* pp. 265-266.
42. *Ibid.,* pp. 289-290.
43. Conversation with Mr. Lippmann, Oct. 31, 1946. See T. and T., Mar. 28, 1935 for an acknowledgment by Lippmann of "the cumbersome process of litigation."
44. *Good Society,* pp. 278-281.
45. *Ibid.,* p. 274.
46. *Ibid.,* p. 223.
47. *Ibid.,* pp. 268-269.
48. *Ibid.,* p. 279.
49. Conversation with Mr. Lippmann, Oct. 31, 1946. See *Good Society,* p. 293.
50. *Good Society,* pp. 203-240.
51. *Ibid.,* p. 227.
52. *Ibid.,* pp. 300-302.
53. *Ibid.,* pp. 298-299.
54. *Ibid.,* pp. 284-285.

CHAPTER FOUR

1. For the theory see Douglas Waples, Bernard Berelson, and Franklin R. Bradshaw, *What Reading Does to People* (Chicago, University of Chicago Press, 1940), 222 pp.
2. T. and T., Jan. 8, 1932.
3. T. and T., Apr. 28, 1932.
4. T. and T., Jun. 7, 1932.
5. T. and T., Apr. 1, 1937.
6. T. and T., Sept. 27, 1932.
7. T. and T., Oct. 7, 1932.
8. T. and T., Nov. 1, 1932.
9. T. and T., Jan. 17, 24; Feb. 10, 14, 17, 24, 1933.
10. T. and T., Jan. 24, 1933.
11. T. and T., Feb. 14, 1933.

12. T. and T., Feb. 28, 1933.
13. T. and T., Mar. 15, 1933.
14. T. and T., Feb. 1, 1934.
15. T. and T., Feb. 27, 1934.
16. T. and T., Jul. 26, 1934.
17. T. and T., Jan. 5, 1935. On Lippmann's opposition to the dole see T. and T., Dec. 11, 25 and 27, 1934; Jan. 19, 1935.
18. T. and T., Jul. 4, 1935.
19. T. and T., Mar. 14, 1935.
20. T. and T., Dec. 14, 1935. Cf. T. and T., Apr. 21, 1938. Supporters of the Administration measure were greatly disturbed by Lippmann's stand. See Heywood Broun, "It Seems to Me," New York *World Telegram*, Dec. 23, 1935; also John T. Flynn, "Other People's Money," *New Republic*, Vol. LXXXVIII (Sept. 23, 1936), pp. 183-184.
21. T. and T., Jul. 18, 1935. Mr. Roosevelt's tax message had gone to Congress on Jun. 19, 1935.
22. T. and T., Aug. 20, 1935.
23. T. and T., Dec. 14, 1935.
24. T. and T., Apr. 18, 1936.
25. T. and T., Dec. 25, 1934; Jan. 5, 19, 1935.
26. T. and T., Apr. 18, 30, 1936.
27. T. and T., May 28, 1936; see also T. and T., Feb. 27, 1936.
28. T. and T., Jun. 23, 1936.
29. T. and T., Jun. 30, 1936.
30. T. and T., Oct. 20, 1936. See also T. and T., Sept. 8, 1936.
31. T. and T., Oct. 7, 1932.
32. T. and T., Oct. 13, 1936.
33. T. and T., Oct. 1, 8, 1936.
34. T. and T., Oct. 8, 1936.
35. T. and T., Oct. 20, 1936.
36. T. and T., Oct. 22, 1936.
37. T. and T., Nov. 5, 1936.
38. T. and T., Nov. 7, 1936.
39. T. and T., Nov. 5, 1936.
40. New York *Herald Tribune*, Mar. 5, 1937.
41. T. and T., Feb. 13, 1937.
42. T. and T., Feb. 23, 1937.
43. T. and T., May 20, 1937.
44. T. and T., Jan. 9, 1937.
45. T. and T., Feb. 18, 1937.
46. T. and T., Mar. 2, 1937.
47. T. and T., Mar. 9, 1937.
48. *Ibid.*
49. T. and T., Jun. 26, 1937.

50. T. and T., May 4, 1937.
51. T. and T., Jul. 15, 1937.
52. T. and T., May 6, 1937.
53. T. and T., Oct. 21, 1937. See also T. and T., Mar. 27, 1937, and Lippmann's "Rise of Personal Government in the United States," *Vital Speeches*, Vol. III (May 1, 1937), pp. 418+.
54. T. and T., Nov. 13, 1937.
55. T. and T., Jan. 11, 1938.

CHAPTER FIVE

1. T. and T., Apr. 6, 1934.
2. T. and T., Jun. 29, 1934.
3. T. and T., Dec. 18, 1934.
4. T. and T., Jan. 8, 1935.
5. T. and T., Apr. 6, 1935.
6. T. and T., Jun. 8, 1935.
7. T. and T., Mar. 19, 1936.
8. T. and T., Jun. 12, 1936.
9. T. and T., Jun. 18, 1936.
10. "Two Conventions in Perspective," broadcast on Jun. 28, 1936; published in *Vital Speeches*, Vol. II (Jul. 15, 1936), pp. 651-653.
11. T. and T., Oct. 13, 22, 1936.
12. T. and T., Jul. 1, 1937.
13. T. and T., Mar. 26, 1938.
14. T. and T., Dec. 19, 1933.
15. T. and T., Mar. 28, 1934.
16. T. and T., Jul. 27, 1935.
17. T. and T., Jan. 9, 1936.
18. T. and T., Jan. 14, 1936.
19. T. and T., May 28, 1936.
20. T. and T., Jul. 26, 27; Nov. 3, 1933.
21. T. and T., Nov. 7, 1933.
22. T. and T., Mar. 2, 22, 1934.
23. T. and T., Mar. 22, 23; Jun. 7, 1934; May 29, 1935.
24. T. and T., Mar. 27, 1934.
25. T. and T., Dec. 4, 1934.
26. T. and T., Mar. 1, 1935.
27. T. and T., Mar. 19, 1936. See also T. and T., Aug. 7, Dec. 31, 1937; Mar. 26 and May 3, 1938.
28. T. and T., Nov. 12, 1936.
29. T. and T., Feb. 25, 1936.
30. T. and T., Jan. 25, 1938.
31. T. and T., Mar. 8, 24, 26; Nov. 29, 1938.
32. T. and T., Aug. 3, 1933.

33. T. and T., Mar. 21, 1934.

34. T. and T., Mar. 22, 23; Jun. 7, 1934.

35. T. and T., Mar. 28, 1935.

36. T. and T., May 21, 1935. See also T. and T., Mar. 21, 1935.

37. T. and T., Mar. 28, 1935.

38. T. and T., Jan. 12, 1937.

39. T. and T., Feb. 20, 1937. See also T. and T., Jan. 30, 1937.

40. T. and T., Jun. 24, 1937.

41. Walter Lippmann, *The New Imperative,* p. 1.

42. T. and T., May 30, 1934.

43. T. and T., Jan. 19, 1935.

44. T. and T., Apr. 20, 1935.

45. T. and T., Apr. 20, 27, 1935.

46. Walter Lippmann, "Security," *American Magazine,* Vol. CXIX (May, 1935), pp. 71+. See also T. and T., Apr. 27, 1935.

47. T. and T., Dec. 12, 1935; Feb. 27, 1936.

48. T. and T., Jan. 21, 1936.

49. T. and T., May 28, 1936.

50. T. and T., Dec. 12, 1935.

51. T. and T., May 9, 1935.

52. T. and T., May 30, 1934; Jan. 19, 1935. See also his "Security," *loc. cit.,* pp. 71+.

53. New York *Herald Tribune,* Mar. 1, 1937.

54. T. and T., May 28, 1936.

55. *U.S. War Aims,* p. 199.

56. T. and T., Sept. 18, 1945.

57. T. and T., May 29, 1937. See also T. and T., Jul. 31, 1937.

58. T. and T., Jun. 26, 1937.

59. T. and T., Aug. 3, 5, 1937.

60. T. and T., May 21, 1938.

CHAPTER SIX

1. *Preface to Politics,* pp. 184-185.

2. *Drift and Mastery,* p. 72.

3. *Ibid.,* pp. 75-76.

4. *Ibid.,* p. 23.

5. *Drift and Mastery,* pp. 45-49. See also Lippmann's "Big Business Men of Tomorrow," *American Magazine,* Vol. CXVII (Apr. 1934), pp. 18+.

6. *Drift and Mastery,* p. 60.

7. *Ibid.,* p. 50.

8. *Preface to Morals,* p. 257.

9. "Big Business Men of Tomorrow," *loc cit.,* pp. 18+. Cf. Amos Pinchot, "The Great Elucidator," *Nation,* Vol. CXXXVII (Jul. 5, 1933), pp. 7-10, and *Method of Freedom,* pp. 100-101.

10. "Big Business Men of Tomorrow," *loc. cit.,* pp. 18+.
11. *Drift and Mastery,* p. 254.
12. *Method of Freedom,* p. 96.
13. *Ibid.,* pp. 100-102.
14. *Preface to Morals,* p. 254.
15. T. and T., Apr. 28, 1933.
16. *Men of Destiny,* p. 109.
17. T. and T., Sept. 6, 1932.
18. T. and T., Jan. 26; Feb. 16, 1933.
19. T. and T., Mar. 9, 1933.
20. T. and T., Mar. 29, 1933. See also T. and T., Apr. 11, 18, 19, 1933.
21. T. and T., Apr. 18, 1933.
22. T. and T., Apr. 28, 1932.
23. T. and T., May 6, 1932.
24. T. and T., Nov. 7, 1933.
25. T. and T., May 28, 1936.
26. T. and T., Sept. 20, 1935.
27. T. and T., Nov. 24, 1936.
28. "Two Conventions in Perspective," *loc. cit.*
29. T. and T., Jun. 18, 1936.
30. T. and T., Oct. 20, 1936.
31. *Time,* Vol. XXXIV (Nov. 27, 1939), p. 13.
32. T. and T., Mar. 21, 1934.
33. T. and T., Jun. 7, 1934; Feb. 7, 1935.
34. T. and T., Jun. 7, 1934.
35. T. and T., Mar. 21; May 21, 1935.
36. T. and T., Mar. 28, 1935.
37. *Ibid.*
38. T. and T., May 21, 1935.
39. (Boston, Little, Brown, 1943), 177 pp.
40. *U.S. Foreign Policy,* pp. vii-x.
41. *Stakes of Diplomacy* (New York, Macmillan, 1915), p. 226. See also his *Political Scene* (New York, Holt, 1919), pp. 51-52; T. and T., Jan. 6, 1932; and his "America's Great Mistake," *Life,* Vol. XI (Jul. 21, 1941), pp. 74.
42. *Stakes of Diplomacy,* p. 127.
43. *Ibid.,* pp. 156-157.
44. See "The Case for Wilson," *New Republic,* Vol. VIII (Oct. 14, 1916), pp. 263-264, also *Political Scene,* p. 61, and "The Democratic Platform: A Return to Woodrow Wilson," Lippmann's column for Jul. 1, 1932.
45. *Political Scene,* pp. 54-65.
46. *Ibid.,* pp. 98-99.
47. *U.S. War Aims,* p. 180.

48. *Ibid.*, pp. 178-180.
49. *Ibid.*, p. 173.
50. *Ibid.*, pp. 171-172.
51. *Ibid.*, pp. 161; 164-165; 187.
52. *Ibid.*, pp. 165-167.
53. *Ibid.*, p. 99.
54. *Ibid.*, pp. 187, 190-191.
55. *Ibid.*, p. 191.
56. (New York, Harper and Bros., 1947), 62 pp.
57. Walter Lippmann, "Philosophy and United States Foreign Policy," *Vital Speeches*, Vol. XIV (Feb. 1, 1948), pp. 242-244.

CHAPTER SEVEN

1. *Preface to Politics*, pp. 57, 59.
2. *Drift and Mastery*, p. 23.
3. *Ibid.*, p. 9.
4. *Ibid.*, p. 25.
5. *Ibid.*, pp. 45-59.
6. "Big Business Men of Tomorrow," *loc. cit.*, pp. 18-19. See also T. and T., "Morals in Business," Dec. 29, 1933.
7. *Preface to Politics*, pp. 184-185; *Drift and Mastery*, pp. 77-100.
8. Chap. IV. See T. and T., Sept. 27; Oct. 7, 1932.
9. T. and T., Feb. 21, 1935.
10. T. and T., Apr. 4, 1935.
11. T. and T., Mar. 14, 1935. See also *Good Society*, pp. 216-217. He partially compromised his position in columns of Jul. 4 and Dec. 14, 1935.
12. T. and T., Jul. 13, 1934.
13. T. and T., Jun. 25, 1935.
14. *New Republic*, Vol. I (Jan. 30, 1915), pp. 12-13.
15. Pp. 59-60, 64-65.
16. P. 101.
17. *Method of Freedom*, p. 113.
18. *Ibid.*, pp. 103-105.
19. T. and T., Dec. 29, 1932.
20. T. and T., Jul. 18, 1935.
21. T. and T., Jun. 25, 1935.
22. T. and T., Feb. 27, 1936; *Time*, Vol. XXXIX (May 11, 1942), p. 15.
23. T. and T., Apr. 12, 1935; May 28, 1936. For an elaboration of Lippmann's tax views see *Good Society*, pp. 226-228.
24. T. and T., Mar. 14, 1935.
25. T. and T., Dec. 14, 1935.
26. T. and T., Dec. 21, 1935.

27. Chap. VI. Cf. *Method of Freedom*, pp. 107-109; *Good Society*, pp. 203-240.

28. *Method of Freedom*, p. 109.

29. Pp. 45-57.

30. 1st ed., p. vii.

31. *Ibid.*

32. *Ibid.*, p. xii.

33. T. and T., Feb. 10; Jun. 18; Oct. 7; Nov. 2, 4, 1932. See also "Reckoning: Twelve Years of Republican Rule," *Yale Review*, Vol. XXI (Jun., 1932), pp. 649-660.

34. T. and T., Apr. 13, 1933; May 30, 1935; Apr. 30, 1936.

35. T. and T., May 26; Oct. 6, 1932. See also Lippmann's "The Permanent New Deal," *Yale Review*, Vol. XXIV (Jun., 1935), pp. 649-667.

36. Chap. IV; See T. and T., Feb. 10; Jun. 15; Jul. 13, 1932; Jul. 10, 1934.

37. *Good Society*, pp. 222-223.

38. Speech before the New Council of American Business, Chicago, Ill., Dec. 11, 1946.

39. Max Lerner, "Lippmann Agonistes," *Nation*, Vol. CXLV (Nov. 27, 1937), pp. 589-590.

40. Margaret Marshall, "Columnists on Parade," *National*, Vol. CXLVI (April 23, 1938), pp. 464-467.

41. *Public Opinion*, p. 273.

42. *Ibid.*, p. 120.

43. *Ibid.*, p. 364.

44. *Ibid.*, pp. 380-383.

45. *Ibid.*, p. 370.

46. *Phantom Public*, p. 39.

47. *Ibid.*, pp. 42-44. In conversation with the writer, Oct. 31, 1946, Mr. Lippmann spoke of the present need for "fact-finders."

48. *Public Opinion*, pp. 56-57, 61-62.

49. *Phantom Public*, pp. 67-71, 146-148.

50. *Ibid.*, pp. 68, 138-139, 145.

51. "Why Should the Majority Rule?" *Harpers*, Vol. CLII (Mar., 1926), p. 403.

52. *Phantom Public*, p. 58.

53. *American Inquisitors* (New York, Macmillan, 1928), p. 11.

54. *Method of Freedom*, p. 76.

55. *Phantom Public*, p. 58. T. and T., Nov. 26, 1936.

56. T. and T., Nov. 26, 1936. See also *Good Society*, p. 107.

57. T. and T., Jan. 25, 1936.

58. *Phantom Public*, p. 155.

59. *Preface to Morals*, p. 326.

60. *Ibid.*, p. 137.

61. *Ibid.*, p. 221.

62. *Ibid.*, pp. 218-220.

63. *Ibid.*, p. 329.

64. T. and T., May 20, 1932.

65. "Scholar in a Troubled World," *loc. cit.*, pp. 148-152.

66. *Good Society*, pp. 383-389.

67. "Walter Lippman's Evolution," Vol. XXX (Aug. 4, 1939), pp. 348-350. See a praiseful editorial about Lippmann, "Spiritual Revolution," *Commonweal*, Vol. XXIII (Mar. 13, 1936), pp. 533-534, and L. J. A. Mercier, "Columnists and Professors," *Commonweal*, Vol. XXXI (Jan. 26, 1940), pp. 296-298.

68. "State of Education in this Troubled Age," *Vital Speeches*, Vol. VII (Jan. 15, 1941), pp. 200-203.

69. *Good Society*, p. 230.

70. "Man's Image of Man," *Commonweal*, Vol. XXXV (Feb. 13, 1942), pp. 406-409. An address to the American Catholic Philosophical Association.

71. "Man's Image of Man," p. 406.

72. *Ibid.*, p. 408.

CHAPTER EIGHT

1. (New York, Macmillan, 1932), Allan Nevins, Ed., 361 pp.

2. William Allen White, "Walter Lippmann Looks at the Political Scene," New York *Herald Tribune*, Oct. 23, 1932.

3. Quoted from the *Emporia Gazette* in the New York *Herald Tribune*, Sept. 8, 1931.

4. "Walter Lippmann," New York *Herald Tribune* (Sept. 11, 1932).

5. "Walter Lippmann," *Saturday Review of Literature*, Vol. IX (Jan. 7, 1933), pp. 361-362.

6. Unable to restrain themselves when they have a good story to tell, no matter who the victim, *Time* related this: "Sharpest dig at Walter Lippmann was made by Mabel Dodge Luhan, whose Manhattan *salon* Lippmann frequented as a young man: 'Walter is never going to lose an eye in a fight. He might lose his glow, but he will never lose an eye.'" *Time*, Vol. XXX (Sept. 27, 1937), p. 47.

7. *Time*, Vol. XXX (Sept. 27, 1937), pp. 45-48.

8. "Spiritual Revolution," *loc. cit.*, Vol. XXIII (Mar. 13, 1936), pp. 533-534.

9. *Loc. cit.*, Vol. XXX (Aug. 4, 1939), pp. 348-350.

10. Mercier, "Columnists and Professors," *Commonweal*, Vol. XXI (Jan. 26, 1940), pp. 296-298.

11. "Scholar in a Troubled World," *loc. cit.*, pp. 148-152.

12. "Ivory Tower or Battlefield?" *Christian Century*, Vol. XLIX (Jun. 22, 1932), pp. 790-791.

13. "What Has Happened to Walter Lippmann?" *Christian Century*, Vol. LIII (Sept. 23, 1936), pp. 1245-1246.

14. "Mr. Lippmann's Twisted Morality," *Christian Century*, Vol. LXII (Feb. 20, 1946), pp. 231-232.

15. "Walter Lippmann: The Career of Comrade Fool," *loc. cit.*, p. 273.

16. *Ibid.*, p. 274.

17. Vol. CXXXVII (Jul. 5, 1933), pp. 7-10. The Herald Tribune Syndicate had published a promotion pamphlet about Lippmann in which it had somewhat extravagantly referred to the columnist as "The Great Elucidator." Critics of Lippmann have from time to time revived the appellation.

18. *Loc. cit.*, p. 7.

19. *Nation*, Vol. CXXXVII (Jul. 12, 1933), pp. 36-38.

20. *Nation*, Vol. CXXXVII (Jul. 19, 1933), pp. 66-70.

21. *Loc. cit.*, p. 68.

22. "On Democracy," Vol. CXXXVII (Aug. 2, 1933), pp. 126-131.

23. *Loc. cit.*, p. 128.

24. *Loc. cit.*, pp. 130-131.

25. "Liberal Position," *North American Review*, Vol. CCXLIV (Dec. 1937), pp. 368-388.

26. "Walter Lippmann and Soviet Russia," *New Masses*, Vol. XVI (Aug. 20, 1935), pp. 15-16.

27. *New Masses*, Vol. XXV (Nov. 2, 1937), p. 23. In his volume *You Might Like Socialism* (New York, McLeod, 1939, 308 pp.) Lamont refuted, point by point, the *Good Society* thesis.

28. Vol. XXXVI, pp. 11-12.

29. *New Masses*, Vol. XLVII (Jun. 29, 1943), pp. 15-17.

30. "Other People's Money," *New Republic*, Vol. LXXXVIII (Sept. 23, 1936), pp. 183-184.

31. "Mr. Lippmann and a National Government," *New Republic*, Vol. LXXXVIII (Sept. 23, 1936), pp. 180-181.

32. "It Seems to Me," New York *World Telegram*, Nov. 21, 1933.

33. "It Seems to Me," New York *World Telegram*, Nov. 27, 1936.

34. "Lippmann and the Court," *Nation*, Vol. CXLIV (Feb. 27, 1937), p. 230.

35. "Lippmann Agonistes," *Nation*, Vol. CXLV (Nov. 27, 1937), pp. 589-590.

36. "Columnists on Parade," *Nation*, Vol. CXLVI (Apr. 23, 1938), pp. 464-467.

37. "Walter Lippmann and Educational Reconstruction," *School and Society*, Vol. LVI (Sept. 5, 1942), pp. 169-173. See also J. C. Aldrich, "Lippmann Retreats to Yesterday," *Scholastic*, Vol. XXXVIII (Mar. 17, 1941), p. 1-T.

CHAPTER NINE

1. "The Great Elucidator," *loc. cit.*

2. Conversation with Mr. Lippmann, Oct. 31, 1946.

3. Much more realistic was Lippmann's discussion of trusts in *Preface to Politics*, pp. 22-23, where he showed that monopolies were increasing.

4. See Chap. III.

5. (With Charles Merz) *New Republic* supplement, Vol. XXIII (Aug. 4, 1920), 42 pp. This extraordinary investigation, painstakingly documented, exposed the treatment given by *The New York Times* to critical events in the Russian Revolution.

6. (New York, Harcourt, Brace and Howe), 104 pp.

7. *Commonweal*, Vol. XXXV (Feb. 13, 1942), pp. 406-409.

SELECTED BIBLIOGRAPHY

The bulk of research for this study was based on Walter Lippmann's New York *Herald Tribune* column, "Today and Tomorrow," referred to in the footnotes as "T. and T." These columns have been painstakingly indexed and catalogued by Robert O. Anthony, curator of the Lippmann collection now housed at the Yale University Library. The indexes may be used there by qualified researchers with permission.

For this investigation all columns that dealt with domestic issues in the years 1932 through 1938 were read. See the text for full documentation. Additional sources used are as follows:

BOOKS BY WALTER LIPPMANN

American Inquisitors. New York, Macmillan, 1928. 120 pp.
The Cold War. New York, Harper and Bros, 1947. 62 pp.
Drift and Mastery. New York, Holt, 1914. 334 pp.
The Good Society. Boston, Little, Brown, 1937. 402 pp.
Interpretations 1931-1932. (Allan Nevins, Ed.). New York, Macmillan, 1932. 361 pp.
Interpretations 1933-1935. (Allan Nevins, Ed.). New York, Macmillan, 1936. 399 pp.
Liberty and the News. New York, Harcourt, Brace and Howe, 1920. 104 pp.
Men of Destiny. New York, Macmillan, 1927. 244 pp.
The Method of Freedom. New York, Macmillan, 1934. 117 pp.
The New Imperative. New York, Macmillan, 1935. 52 pp.
The Phantom Public. New York, Harcourt, 1925. 205 pp.
The Political Scene. New York, Holt, 1919. 124 pp.
A Preface to Morals. New York, Macmillan, 1929. 348 pp.

A Preface to Politics. New York, Macmillan, 1933 (1913). 318 pp.

Public Opinion. New York, Macmillan, 1922. 427 pp.

The Stakes of Diplomacy. New York, Macmillan, 1915. 235 pp.

U.S. Foreign Policy: Shield of the Republic. Boston, Little Brown, 1943. 177 pp.

U.S. War Aims. Boston, Little, Brown, 1944. 235 pp.

ARTICLES BY WALTER LIPPMANN

"America's Great Mistake." *Life,* Vol. XI (July 21, 1941), pp. 74+.

"The Apple Woman." *Red and Blue,* Vol. VIII (April, 1904), p. 8.

"Big Business Men of Tomorrow." *American Magazine,* Vol. CXVII (April, 1934), pp. 18+.

"The Campaign Against Sweating." *New Republic,* Vol. II (March 27, 1915), pp. 1-8.

"The Case for Wilson." *New Republic,* Vol. VIII (October 14, 1916), pp. 263-264.

"Deepest Issue of Our Time." *Vital Speeches,* Vol. II (July 1, 1936), pp. 602-604.

"The Discussion of Socialism." *Harvard Illustrated Magazine,* Vol. XI (April, 1910), pp. 231-232.

"England and the English." *Harvard Illustrated Magazine,* Vol. XI (December, 1909), pp. 105-106.

"A Grave." *Red and Blue,* Vol. VIII (March, 1904), p. 18.

"In Defense of the Suffragettes." *Harvard Monthly,* Vol. XLIX (November, 1909), pp. 64-67.

"Life Is Cheap." *New Republic,* Vol. I (December 19, 1914), pp. 12-14.

"Man's Image of Man." *Commonweal,* Vol. XXXV (February 13, 1942), pp. 406-409.

"A Night in a Venetian Palace." *Red and Blue,* Vol. VIII (January, 1904), pp. 10-11.

"Notes for a Biography," *New Republic,* Vol. LXIII (July 16, 1930), pp. 250-252.

"An Open Mind: William James." *Everybody's,* Vol. XXIII (December, 1910), pp. 800-801.

"The Permanent New Deal." *Yale Review,* Vol. XXIV (June, 1935), pp. 649-667.

"Philosophy and United States Foreign Policy." *Vital Speeches,* Vol. XIV (Feb. 1, 1948), pp. 242-244.
"Problem in Imperceptibles." *Harvard Monthly,* Vol. XLIX (December, 1909), pp. 95-98.
"Providential State." *Atlantic,* Vol. CLVIII (October, 1936), pp. 403-412.
"Reckoning: Twelve Years of Republican Rule." *Yale Review,* Vol. XXI (June, 1932), pp. 649-660.
"Rise of Personal Government in the United States." *Vital Speeches,* Vol. III (May 1, 1937), pp. 418+.
"Scholar in a Troubled World." *Atlantic,* Vol. CL (August, 1932), pp. 148-152.
"Security." *American Magazine,* Vol. CXIX (May, 1935), pp. 71+.
"Socialism at Harvard." *Harvard Illustrated Magazine,* Vol. X (March, 1909), pp. 137-139.
"State of Education in this Troubled Age." *Vital Speeches,* Vol. VII (January 15, 1941), pp. 200-203.
"A Test of the News." *New Republic Supplement,* Vol. XXIII (August 4, 1920), 42 pp. With Charles Merz.
"Two Conventions in Perspective." *Vital Speeches,* Vol. II (July 15, 1936), pp. 651-653.
"Two Months in Schenectady." *The Masses,* Vol. III (April, 1912), p. 13.
"Walter Lippman." *Harvard College Class of 1910,* Twenty-fifth Anniversary Report. Cosmos Press. Cambridge, Mass. 1935, pp. 446-449.
"Why Should the Majority Rule?" *Harpers,* Vol. CLII (March, 1926), pp. 399-405.

BOOKS AND ARTICLES ABOUT WALTER LIPPMANN

Adams, James Truslow. "Walter Lippman." *Saturday Review of Literature,* Vol. IX (January 7, 1933), pp. 361-362.
Aldrich, J. C. "Lippman Retreats to Yesterday." *Scholastic,* Vol. XXXVIII (March 17, 1941), p. 1-T.
Bates, Ernest Sutherland. "Walter Lippman: The Career of Comrade Fool." *Modern Monthly,* Vol. VII (June, 1933), pp. 266-274.
Blankenhorn, Heber. *Adventures in Propaganda.* Boston, Houghton, Mifflin, 1919. 167 pp.

Bliven, Bruce. "Mr. Lippman and a National Government." *New Republic,* Vol. XXXVIII (September 23, 1936), pp. 180-181.

Brandl, Cecelia M. *Mr. Walter Lippmann's Theory of Political Freedom.* Unpublished Master's thesis. Milwaukee, Marquette University, 1941. 148 pp.

Broun, Heywood. "It Seems to Heywood Broun." *Nation,* Vol. CXXV (September 14, 1927), p. 243.

—— "It Seems to Heywood Broun." *Nation,* Vol. CXXVI (May 4, 1928), p. 532.

—— "It Seems to Me." New York *World-Telegram,* November 22, 1933.

—— "It Seems to Me." New York *World-Telegram,* December 23, 1935.

—— "It Seems to Me." New York *World-Telegram,* November 27, 1936.

Cain, James M. "The End of the 'World.'" *New Freeman,* Vol. II (March 11, 1931), pp. 610-612.

Fisher, Charles. *The Columnists.* New York, Howell, Soskin, 1944. 317 pp.

Flynn, John T. "Other People's Money." *New Republic,* Vol. LXXXVIII (September 23, 1936), pp. 183-184.

Gideonse, Harry D. "Walter Lippmann and Educational Reconstruction." *School and Society,* Vol. LVI (September 5, 1942), pp. 169-173.

Giles, Barbara. "Pundit in a Penthouse." *New Masses,* Vol. XXXVI (September 10, 1940), pp. 11-12.

Giles, Walter I., Jr. *The Contribution of Walter Lippmann to American Political Thought.* Unpublished Master's thesis, Georgetown University, 1945. 212 pp.

Harvard Class Album, 1910. Cambridge, Mass., University Press, 1910. p. 63.

Hicks, Granville. *John Reed.* New York, Macmillan, 1936. 445 pp.

Ickes, Harold L. "Washington Newsmen." *Pageant,* Vol. II (May, 1946), pp. 4-11.

"Ivory Tower or Battlefield?" *Christian Century,* Vol. XLIX (June 22, 1932), pp. 790-791.

Lamont, Corliss. "Walter Lippmann and Soviet Russia." *New Masses,* Vol. XVI (August 20, 1935), pp. 15-16.

—— *You Might Like Socialism.* New York, McLeod, 1939. 308 pp.

Lerner, Max. "Lippmann Agonistes." *Nation,* Vol. CXLV (November 27, 1937), pp. 589-590.

—— "Lippmann and the Court." *Nation,* Vol. CXLIV (February 27, 1937), p. 230.

Marshall, Margaret. "Columnists on Parade." *Nation,* Vol. CXLVI (April 23, 1938), pp. 464-467.

Mercier, L. J. A. "Columnists and Professors." *Commonweal,* Vol. XXXI (January 26, 1940), pp. 296-298.

—— "Walter Lippmann's Evolution." *Commonweal,* Vol. XXX, (August 4, 1939), pp. 348-350.

"Mr. Lippmann's Twisted Morality." *Christian Century,* Vol. LXII (February 20, 1946), pp. 231-232.

Nevins, Allan. "Walter Lippmann." New York *Herald Tribune,* September 11, 1932.

O'Brien, John C. "Lapsed Liberal." *Molders of Opinion,* (David Bulman, Ed.). Milwaukee, Bruce Publishing Co., 1945. 166 pp.

Pinchot, Amos. "The Great Elucidator." *Nation,* Vol. CXXXVII (July 5, 1933), pp. 7-10.

—— "The New Tammany," *Nation,* Vol. CXXXVII (July 12, 1933), pp. 36-38.

—— "Obfuscator de Luxe." *Nation,* Vol. CXXXVII (July 19, 1933), pp. 66-70.

—— "On Democracy." *Nation,* Vol. CXXXVII (August 2, 1933), pp. 126-131.

Public Speaking Memorabilia. A record of Dr. Sach's Collegiate Institute. In possession of Franklin School, 18 West 89th St., New York City.

Rodell, Fred. "Walter Lippmann." *American Mercury,* Vol. LX (March, 1945), pp. 263-273.

Secretary's First Report, Harvard College Class of 1910. Cambridge, Mass., Crumson Printing Co., 1911. p. 41.

Seymour, Charles (Ed.) *The Intimate Papers of Colonel House.* Vol. III, pp. 319-322; Vol. IV, pp. 152-158. New York, Houghton Mifflin, 1938.

Shotwell, James T. *At the Paris Peace Conference.* New York, Macmillan, 1937. pp. 3-19.

"Spiritual Revolution." *Commonweal,* Vol. XXIII (March 13, 1936), pp. 533-534.

Starobin, Joseph. "The Heart of Foreign Policy." *New Masses,* Vol. XLVII (June 29, 1943), pp. 15-17.

Steffens, Lincoln. *Autobiography of Lincoln Steffens.* New York, Harcourt, Brace, 1931. 884 pp.

Time, Vol. XXX (September 27, 1937), pp. 45-48; Vol. XXXII (December 5, 1938), p. 19; Vol. XXXIV (November 27, 1939), p. 13; Vol. XXXIX (May 11, 1942), p. 15; Vol. XLIX (April 7, 1947), p. 27.

Villard, Oswald G. "Walter Lippmann's Prize Piece." *Nation,* Vol. CXLIV (January 16, 1937), p. 72.

"Walter Lippmann." *United Nations World,* Vol. I (May, 1947), p. 19.

"What Has Happened to Walter Lippmann?" *Christian Century,* Vol. LIII (September 23, 1936), pp. 1245-1246.

White, William Allen. "Walter Lippmann Looks at the Political Scene." New York *Herald Tribune,* October 23, 1932.

Williams, Michael. "Inviolable Persons." A review of *Good Society. Commonweal,* October 22, 1937. pp. 609-610.

OTHER REFERENCES USED IN THE STUDY

Advertising Research Foundation. *Continuing Study of Newspaper Reading.* New York, 1946. 64 pp.

Commission on Freedom of the Press. *A Free and Responsible Press.* University of Chicago Press, 1947. 139 pp.

Smith, Bruce L., Lasswell, Harold D., and Casey, Ralph D. *Propaganda, Communications, and Public Opinion.* Princeton University Press, 1946. 435 pp.

"Pundit's Progress." *Fortune,* Vol. XXI (January, 1940), pp. 90-92.

Waples, Douglas, Berelson Bernard, and Bradshaw, Franklyn R. *What Reading Does to People.* University of Chicago Press, 1940. 222 pp.

INDEX

Adams, James Truslow, 110.
Adams, Sam, xiv.
Agenda of Liberalism, 44, 46, 121, 122.
Agricultural Adjustment Act, 54, 55, 57, 62, 63, 64-65, 83, 120.
Albertson, Chrissie, 10.
Albertson, Hazel Hammond, 10.
Albertson, Phyllis, 10.
Albertson, Ralph, 9-10.
American Federation of Labor, 15, 85.
American Geographical Society, 15, 16.
American-Russian relations, 17, 90-91.
Anderson, Benjamin M., 34.
Army and Navy Club, 24.
Army-Navy Country Club, 24.
Arnheim, Sam, 5.
"A Test of the News," 126.
Atlantic Pact, 90, 91.
Atomic bomb, 91.

Baker, Newton D., 15, 49.
Baltimore Sun, 29.
Bates, Ernest Sutherland, 11, 111.
Bennett, James Gordon, xiv.
Berge, Wendell, 99.
Binger, Carl, 5, 10.
Binger, Walter, 10.

Bliven, Bruce, 114.
Bolsheviks, 16.
Bonnet, Henri, 25.
Borah, William E., 53, 58.
Boston Common, 10, 11.
Bowman, Isaiah, 15, 16.
Braden, Spruille, 25.
Broun, Heywood, 19, 32, 114.
Bureaucracy, 43, 44, 45, 46, 122.

Cain, James M., 19, 20, 27.
Carter, Boake, 32.
Catholic Church, 105, 106, 107, 111.
Century Club, 24.
Chestnut Hill Farm, 10.
Christian Century, 111.
Circolo Italiano, 7.
Civil Service House, 7.
Civilian Conservation Corps, 37.
Civil Works Administration, 37.
Cobb, Frank, 17, 18, 20.
Coffee House Club, 24.
Cold War, The, 90.
Collectivism, 35, 38, 39, 40, 41, 42, 46, 52, 54, 60, 63, 65, 74, 83, 98, 99, 105, 123, 127.
Collier, Price, 7.
Column writers, xi-xii, xiii, xiv.
Commission on Freedom of the Press, 30, 125, 126.
Commonweal, 105, 110.